W9-ACI-825

Days with Walt Whitman

*

GEORGE · ALLEN ·
PUBLISHER · LONDON ·
RUSKIN · HOUSE
156 · CHARING · CROSS · ROAD ·

Allen & Co. Sc.

Walt Whitman
at the age of 35

Days with Walt Whitman

With some Notes on his Life and Work

By Edward Carpenter

London: George Allen, *Ruskin House*
156 Charing Cross Road   Mdccccvi

SECOND EDITION

Printed by BALLANTYNE, HANSON & Co.
At the Ballantyne Press

PREFACE

MY first acquaintance with Whitman's writings (William Rossetti's edition of the Poems) was made at Cambridge during the Long Vacation in the summer of 1868—or it may have been '69. But it was not till 1877 that I crossed the Atlantic and paid my first visit to him. In 1884 I was again in the States, and saw Whitman several times. The notes made on the occasions of these visits were written out at a later period, and finally published in the *Progressive Review* (February and April 1897) in the same form as they now stand. The other papers in the present book belong to a still later date, and, with one exception, have not been published before.

E. C.

April 1906.

A VISIT TO WALT WHITMAN IN 1877

A VISIT TO WALT WHITMAN IN 1877

IT was on the 2nd of May 1877, that—crossing the water from Philadelphia—I knocked at the door of 431 Stevens Street, Camden. The house, a narrow three-storied one, stood in one of those broad tree-planted streets which are common in the States; and Whitman was staying there, boarding with his brother Colonel George Whitman and wife—making the establishment at any rate his headquarters, though frequently absent from it. I waited a few minutes in a sitting-room of the usual type—one or two ornamental tables, with photograph books, things under glass shades, &c.—while "Walt" was called upstairs. He soon came down, slowly, leaning heavily on the banisters, always dragging somewhat his paralysed leg—at first sight quite an old man with long grey, almost white, beard, and shaggy head and neck, grey dress too; but tall, erect, and at closer sight not so old—a florid fresh complexion, pure grey-blue eye (no sign of age there), and full, strong, well-formed hands.

At the foot of the staircase he took me by the hand and said, "I was afraid we should miss after all"—this in reference to a previous unsuccessful call I had made. There was no hurry in his manner; having found me a seat, and then only leaving hold of my hand, he sat down himself and asked me "what news I brought from Britain." War had just been declared between Russia and Turkey. Like other

Americans, his sympathies lay with Russia. His idea was that Russia stood *in need* of a southern outlet (Constantinople) for her people and growing energies, that Turkey was falling in pieces, and that England was beginning to pursue "the wise policy of absolute non-intervention." Conversation then turned on England. He asked about friends there; also about myself some questions.

Meanwhile in that first ten minutes I was becoming conscious of an impression which subsequently grew even more marked—the impression, namely, of immense vista or background in his personality. If I had thought before (and I do not know that I had) that Whitman was eccentric, unbalanced, violent, my first interview certainly produced quite a contrary effect. No one could be more considerate, I may almost say courteous; no one could have more simplicity of manner and freedom from egotistic wrigglings; and I never met any one who gave me more the impression of *knowing what he was doing* than he did. Yet away and beyond all this I was aware of a certain radiant power in him, a large benign effluence and inclusiveness, as of the sun, which filled out the place where he was—yet with something of reserve and sadness in it too, and a sense of remoteness and inaccessibility.

Some such impressions, at any rate, I gathered in the first interview. I remember how I was most struck, in his face, by the high arch of the eyebrows, giving a touch of child-like wonder and contemplation to his expression; yet his eyes, though full of a kind of wistful tenderness, were essentially not contemplative but perceptive—active rather than receptive—lying far back, steady, clear, with small definite pupils and heavy lids of passion and experience. A face of majestic simple proportion, like a Greek temple as some one has said; the nose Greek in outline, straight (but not at all thin or narrow, rather the contrary), broad between the brows, and meeting the line of the forehead without any great change of direction; the forehead high, with horizontal furrows, but not excessively high; the head domed, and rising to a great height in the middle, above the ears —not projecting behind; ears large and finely formed; mouth full, but almost quite concealed by hair. A head altogether impressing one by its height, and by a certain untamed "wild hawk" look, not uncommon among the Americans.

After some conversation Whitman proposed a walk across to Philadephia. Putting on his grey slouch hat he sallied forth with evident pleasure, and taking my arm as a support walked slowly the best part of a mile to the ferry. Crossing the ferry was always a great pleasure to him. His "Brooklyn Ferry" and the section entitled "Delaware River —Days and Nights" in "Specimen Days," sufficiently prove this. The life of the streets and of the people was so near, so dear. The men on the ferry steamer were evidently old friends; and when we landed on the Philadelphia side we were before long quite besieged. The man or woman selling fish at the corner of the street, the tramway conductor, the loafers on the pavement—a word of recognition from Walt, or as often from the other first. Presently a cheery shout from the top of a dray; and before we had gone many yards farther the driver was down and standing in front of us—his horses given to the care of some bystander. He was an old Broadway "stager," "had not seen Walt for three or four years"; and tears were in his eyes as he held his hand. We were now brought to a standstill, and others gathered round; "George" was ill, and Walt must go and see him. There was a message for the children, and in his pocket the poet discovered one or two packets of sweetmeats for absent little ones. But for the most part his words were few. It was the others who spoke, and apparently without reserve.

Thus we rambled through Philadelphia—mostly using the tramcars. The Yankees do not walk; the trams in their large towns are very complete, and are universally used for all but short distances. Whitman *could* not walk far. I was content being with him anyhow. He certainly was restfulness itself. When we reached the Ferry on our return, the last bell was ringing—we might have caught the boat, but Whitman seemed not to think of hurrying. The boat went, and he sat down to enjoy life waiting for the next.

A few days later, Walt having gone into the country to stay with his "dear and valued friends," the Staffords, I paid him a visit there. "White Horse," or Kirkwood, was the third or fourth station from Camden on the Camden and Atlantic line; and consisted at that time of only some half-dozen houses and stores, forming a centre to the scattered and outlying farmsteads of that part. The Staffords' little farm lay a mile and a half or so from the station—a five or six-roomed wooden house, a barn, one or two fruit trees, and a few fields running down 300 or 400 yards to a little stream. The country level, very slightly undulating, wooded here and there, not unlike some parts of Cambridgeshire that I have seen—neither particularly attractive or unattractive. Here on this farm, and working it himself, lived Mr. Stafford with his family; he a loyal Methodist, sometimes acting as local preacher, silent-mannered, dark-skinned, of bilious temperament, subject to illness, hard-working, and faithful; his wife a fine woman of cultured expression and spiritual mind, pretty well absorbed in domestic work; two sons, young fellows, one of whom, Harry, at this time working in a printer's office in Camden, was a great ally and favourite of Walt's; a grown-up daughter, and one or two children. Here Whitman would often stay, weeks or months at a time, boarding and living with the family, and attracting the members of it to him, and himself to them, with the ties of enduring friendship. Mrs. Stafford once said to me: "He *is* a good man; I think he is the best man I ever knew."

It was his delight, and doubtless one of

the chief attractions of this favourite resort, to go down and spend a large part of the day by the "creek" which I have spoken of—and which figures so largely in "Specimen Days." At a point not a quarter of a mile distant from the house it widened into a kind of little lake surrounded by trees, the haunt of innumerable birds; and here Whitman would sit for hours in an old chair; silent, enjoying the scene, becoming a part of it, almost, himself; or would undress and bathe in the still, deep pool. At this time he was nearly sixty years old, and for some eight years on and off had been stricken with paralysis. As is well known, he attributed his partial recovery very largely to the beneficence of this creek, with its water-baths and sun-baths and open-air influences generally.

That day being Sunday I found the family all at home, and Whitman in the midst of them. When the opportunity occurred I told him something of the appreciation of his writings that had grown up in England during those years. After a pause he asked if the Rossetti edition was out of print. I said I thought so. W.: "I hope it is; I approved of Rossetti's plan for the time being, but now would rather appear without alteration." [I am here simply transcribing my notes made a day or two after; these are not his exact words, but as good as I could remember.] "I had hardly realised that there was so much interest in me in England. I confess I am surprised that America, to whom I have especially addressed myself, is so utterly silent. Lowell, and indeed almost all the critics, say that I am crude, inartistic—do you think that?" I said I had heard such criticisms, but I did not myself think his work crude and hasty; on the contrary, much of it seemed to me to have been written very deliberately and carefully; and as to the question of art, I thought he had laid an altogether broader basis of style (instancing some of his poems)—a great foundation; others would build here and there upon it, but he had struck the main lines. W.: "I did, in fact, re-write and destroy much before I published; I cannot think that I have altogether attained, but I have planted the seed; it is for others to continue the work. My original idea was that if I could bring men together by putting before them the heart of man, with all its joys and sorrows and experiences and surroundings, it would be a great thing; up to this time I have had America chiefly in view, but this appreciation of me in England makes me think I might perhaps do the same for the old world also. I have endeavoured from the first to get free as much as possible from all literary attitudinising—to strip off integuments, coverings, bridges—and to speak straight from and to the heart." [In reference to this, he said at another time that it had been a "whim" of his when writing "to discard all conventional poetic phrases, and every touch of or reference to ancient or mediæval images, metaphors, subjects, styles, &c., and to write *de novo* with words and phrases appropriate to his own days."]

When we went in to dinner Mr. Stafford was already seated; I think he was about to say grace. Walt, with greater grace, stood for a moment bending over him from behind, and clasped Stafford's head in his great hands; then passed on in silence. What a large sweet presence—so benign, yet so determined! The children loved him, and the little boy would lie coiled, lost, on his knees, half-asleep, half-awake, Walt's hand covering and compressing his entire face.

In Philadelphia, the day before, Whitman had introduced me to his English friends, the Gilchrists. Mrs. Gilchrist, widow of Alexander Gilchrist, the biographer of Blake, was a capable and large-minded woman. A year earlier she, with two daughters and a son, had come from England for a two or three years' visit to the States, and had settled in Philadelphia. As is well known, she was the first of Englishwomen to fully and publicly recognise (as she did in some printed letters) the splendid genius of the poet, and that at a time (1868 or '69) when "Leaves of Grass" to most of the literary world was little better than the incoherent ramblings of a maniac. More than once did she relate to me how, on first opening the volume, when her eye fell upon the fine nearly full-length engraving (taken from a daguerrotype) of the author, she exclaimed: "Here at last is the face of Christ, which the painters have so long sought for"; and she always maintained that the reading of the book itself did but confirm and deepen that first impression.

At the Gilchrists' house Whitman would not unfrequently stay. Indeed there was a kind of prophet's chamber for him there, always ready. And as it happened that he was about to pay a visit there, it was arranged that I also should come. They lived at No. 1929, North 22nd Street. If the American method of numbering streets and houses is prosaic, it certainly has the advantage of being practical. Philadelphia is like a chessboard; you find your way by co-ordinate geometry. The streets are straight, parallel, and not far from infinite in length. The address being put in your hands, you know at once the exact spot to which you are destined.

I remember very well arriving, bag in hand, and finding the whole family (a general custom in Philadelphia on those warm evenings) sitting out on the door-steps—Whitman in the midst, in an arm-chair, his white beard and hair glistening in the young moonlight, looking like some old god—the others grouped around him or at his feet. After this for a week of evenings I made one of the party. How pleasant it was! Whitman had a knack of making ordinary life enjoyable, redeeming it from commonplaceness. Instead of making you feel (as so many do) that the Present is a kind of squalid necessity to be got over as best may be, in view of something always in the future, he gave you that good sense of *nowness*, that faith that the present is enjoyable, which imparts colour and life to the thousand and one dry details of existence. As I have hinted before, he was no great talker, and would generally let the conversation ebb and flow at its own will, without effort, ready apparently for grave or gay alike.

Unlike many highly important people who seem to enjoy holding forth to a general audience, Whitman, as I thought, preferred to let conversation turn on the pivot of personal relationship. Often as not he would have his listener by the hand; and his words too had an attractive force, from their very simplicity and purity from affectation or display. I think he did not really care to have conversational dealings with people except on such a basis of personal affection. To such as he did not like—to all mere gabblers, bores, spying and prying persons—he became as a precipice, instantly and utterly inaccessible. Certainly it was one of the pleasures of his society that you always felt he was there in person, *bonâ fide*, not by deputy; and no current notion of politeness could make him do a thing he did not enjoy doing. One evening we were looking over some fine engravings, mostly portraits, Gainsboroughs, Reynolds, Lelys, and others, from Mrs. Gilchrist's collection. He enjoyed them greatly, and very deliberately, dwelling long and long over some of them, criticising style, workmanship, composition, character, &c. But when he had had enough of it all—well, he said so! I have seldom known any one who, though so cordial and near to others, detached and withdrew himself at times more decisively than he did, or who on the whole spent more time in solitude. Also no rough draft of his character would be complete which did not take into account the strong Quaker element of obstinacy which existed in him—but this might require a separate chapter!

To return to our evenings. I have said something about Walt Whitman's manner in conversation; I cannot attempt to reproduce its effect, but I will just transcribe such notes of some of his remarks as I have by me.

One evening conversation turned upon the Chinese. W.: "I fancy they are like the Germans, only more refined. My notion is that the Germans are simple, true, affectionate folk, but there is a kind of roughness, one may almost say brutishness, about them; the Chinese have the same good qualities, with a certain alertness and grace which the Germans lack." I quoted some accounts of Japan by a man who had lived there for a long time, and who told me that the manners of the old Japanese aristocracy were so elaborately perfect that he himself would go any distance to get *out of their way*, feeling such a boor compared with them! This amused Whitman; seemed to "tally with his own idea." Mrs. Gilchrist wondered, with regard to the natives of India and Orientals generally, that the degradation of the women did not bring about a gradual deterioration of the whole race. W.: "I suppose that among the *masses* of the people the women (and men too) live, after all, much as they do in the West, and as they must do in all times and climes; and that the special treatment of women in the East only applies to the upper classes. The masses in every part of the globe are dominated by the necessities of Nature. Thus also among the Greeks and Romans the peasant-life must have had its races of fine women." And here he cited Juvenal, and his comparison of the effeminate lady of his time with the "stern magnificent mothers" of the early days of Rome.

Going on to Oriental literature, Whitman spoke of "Sakúntala," the Indian drama, its "modernness"—the comic scenes especially being as of the times of Shakespeare; and of the great Hindu epic, the "Ramáyana"; and told the story of Yudísthura, which occurs as an episode in the latter. Conversation got round presently—I think in reference to the cramped life of "high-born" women in the East—to the shoddiness and vulgarity of modern well-to-do life. W.: "It seems a strange thing to me, this love of gilt and upholstery among the Americans—that people leading a free natural open-air life should, directly they make a little money, want to go in for sofas, expensively furnished rooms, dress, and the like; yet it seems to be a law, a kind of necessity, that they should do so.

I suppose it is partly that each man wishes to feel himself as good as others, to feel that he can have of the 'best' too; democracy showing itself for a time in that way, reducing the borrowed old-world standard of superiority to an absurdity; and I guess it will not last for ever."

We did not generally sit up later than eleven. Breakfast was at 7.30 or 8. Walt's arrival in the morning was as exhilarating as a fine sunrise. After breakfast and a chat we would separate to our respective occupations. In the afternoon, almost every day I was there, the poet went off to Camden to visit his sister-in-law, who was at that time confined to the house, and to whom, I believe, he was much attached. As I have said, Walt was very simple and domestic in his ways; and would quite enjoy, on a rainy afternoon, having a game of twenty questions such as he had "often played in camp with the soldiers during the war," or would take pleasure in preparing some little dish of his own devising for the evening meal. One evening we pressed him to read. He would not recite anything of his own; but he read out Tennyson's "Ulysses"—in a clear, strong, and rugged tone. The subtle harmonies of the Tennysonian verse effloresced under the treatment, but the sterner qualities of the poem stood out finely. We expressed admiration. He said: "I guess it is about the best Tennysonian poem." Another evening, I remember, he told us how, when living at New York, he had had a "fancy" to visit Sing-sing prison, the great penal establishment up the Hudson river. He obtained permission to do so, got to know one or two of the warders, and for some time went there pretty frequently. He wrote letters for the prisoners, &c. "It was a whim."

We had a long talk on manual labour. Most of us agreed it would be a good thing for all classes to take part in—not to be left to one class only. Walt maintained with regard to reforms and the like, that it was no good trying to *benefit* people (labouring people for instance) who did not feel the need of any change. "Many people came to me at one time about slavery, and 'wondered' that I was so quiet about it; but, in truth, I felt that abolitionists were making quite noise enough, and that there were other things just as important which had to be attended to." We got talking of Abraham Lincoln—I suppose in reference to slavery—and I mentioned the story that Lincoln went out of his mind and nearly committed suicide over a love affair. Walt, who always was a great admirer of Lincoln, and who knew a good deal about him and his history, gave this a most emphatic denial, saying that Lincoln was "never even near being crazy."

One of the most amusing incidents of my stay occurred one morning shortly after breakfast, when a visiting card was handed in bearing the ominous inscription "Madame Dorbiney D'Aubigné," and was quickly followed by the appearance of an elderly and loquacious little lady. She was one of those detached women with a reticule who travel about the world in quest of anything "interesting." She had been, she told us, all over the States and seen many celebrities, but could not return to Europe without visiting Whitman—and it was only by a piece of luck that she had found out where he was staying. However, it soon began to appear that her interest in Walt was not so great, naturally, as in herself; for after a few preliminary compliments she settled down to tell us all about the wonderful D'Aubigné family to which she belonged. It ramified all over the civilised world, she said; and the name was spelt in ever so many different ways, but they were all branches of the same family, they were all related to each other—as her own name indeed showed. Walt listened in an amused manner, and for about ten minutes was quite decently courteous and patient. Then I suddenly perceived that his face was becoming 'precipitous'; the little woman of course was addressing him, no one else being of any importance; but he seemed to be becoming deaf, there was no speculation in his eyes; it *was* rather awful; for a minute or two she tried vainly to effect a lodgment for her words, to get any kind of handhold on the sheer surface, and then gathering up her tackle, she made the best of a bad job, bade a hasty good-bye, and disappeared.

I told Walt about a visit I paid to Oliver Wendell Holmes, and the criticisms of "Leaves of Grass" which I heard on that occasion. I saw the "Autocrat of the Breakfast Table" at his house in Boston. He was then about 70 years of age—a dapper active little man, full of life and go, rather enjoying the visits of strangers —"Oh yes, I have a large 'parish'—people write to me and come and call from all parts of the world—we authors are rather vain, you know, and quite enjoy a little homage; but *my* parish is not as big as Longfellow's—not as big as Longfellow's. But this is not a good time for you to see Boston. Boston is very empty now—(getting up and glancing through the window) very empty; you might almost see a fox run down the street; &c., &c." I said something about American literature and "Leaves of Grass." "Oh! Whitman," he said, "well—well—well—Whitman is all very well—he has capacity, but it won't do—it won't do. I tell you what, it's something like this: you know, skilful cooks say that the faintest odour, the merest whiff, of *assa-fœtida*, will give a piquant flavour to a dish—and I can believe that; but to *drench* it in *assafœtida*, no, that won't do. The poets *coquette* with Nature and weave garlands of roses for her; but Whitman *goes at her* like a great hirsute man—no, it won't do. Now," he continued, "the other day Lowell and Longfellow and I were chatting together, and the subject of Whitman turned up. Said Lowell, 'I can't think why there is all this stir about Whitman; I have read a good deal of his poetry, but I can't see anything in it—*I can't see anything in it.*' 'Well,' said Longfellow, 'I believe the man might have done something if he had only had a decent training and education.' As to my own opinion, why," said Holmes, "I have already given you that. So you see what we think of him in America." Whitman was a good deal amused, and took it all in good part, saying he knew pretty well already what they thought.

As the days went by I began to see more clearly the depths which lay behind the poet's simple and unconcerned exterior. Literary persons, as a rule, write over their own heads; they talk a little bigger than themselves. But Whitman seemed to fill out "Leaves of Grass," and form an interpretation of it. I began to see that all he had written there was matter of absolute personal experience—that you might be sure that what was said was meant. There was the same deliberate suggestiveness about his actions and manners that you find in his writings —only, of course, with the added force of bodily presence; and far down too there were clearly enough visible the same strong and contrary moods, the same strange omnivorous egotism, controlled and restrained by that wonderful genius of his for human affection and love. "Who has the most enamoured body?" were words which somehow his presence often suggested. It was with real reluctance that, a week after my arrival, I bade adieu to all that friendly household; and the next morning but one, from the stern of the *Siberia*, watched the flat shores of New England, and the lighthouse that marks the entrance to Boston Harbour, recede and dip below the broadening waters of the Atlantic.

WALT WHITMAN IN 1884

WALT WHITMAN IN 1884

THE next time I saw Walt Whitman was the 17th June 1884. He had then left Stevens Street, owing to the removal of his brother, but was still living in Camden, in a small house which he had himself part-purchased—328 Mickle Street. He had at that time, for housekeepers, an elderly workman and his wife, Mr. and Mrs. Lay, with whom he was on easy terms, and with whom he had his meals. In appearance I thought him much the same as in 1877—a trifle thinner perhaps, and certainly more infirm. Some expression of weariness too I thought I saw, which would likely arise from the increased confinement of his life. "I keep going," he said, "much the same. Visits from English friends are perhaps my chief diversion." Then, after tender inquiries, especially for Mrs. Gilchrist (who was now in London), "have just had a visit from Oscar Wilde—who told me about England; I made him do the talking—rather liked him. I have occasional letters from Dowden—a steady friend—and others. Bucke's book[1] is going off slowly—not much cared for by my friends—but I like it. I opposed the book all along, till Bucke, getting fairly out of patience, came one day and said, 'Now I am just as obstinate as you, and I *intend* to bring it out whether you like it or no—so you had better make the best of the matter and help to make it authentic as far as you can'; whereupon I caved in,

1 "Walt Whitman," by R. Maurice Bucke, M.D. Philadelphia, 1883.

laughing heartily, and wrote the account of my birthplace and antecedents which occupies the first twenty-four pages of the book."

"I thought that there was a germinal idea in Bucke's book—the idea that 'Leaves of Grass' was above all an expression of the Moral Nature. As to O'Connor's letters—I must say I like them. They are comforting. Just as any woman likes a man to fall in love with her—whether she returns it or not—so to have once aroused so eloquent and passionate a declaration is reassuring and a help to me." We then spoke of the money-making and gentility business at New York—I remarking that I thought it had all increased considerably since I was there in '77, and he corroborating, though holding that it probably *had* to be gone through "for reasons."

Here I find the following passage

among my notes: "I am impressed more than ever with W.'s contradictory, self-willed, tenacious, obstinate character, strong and even extreme moods, united with infinite tenderness, wistful love, and studied tolerance; also great caution [he says: 'the phrenologists always say that caution is my chief characteristic—did you know that?'] and a certain artfulness, combined with keen, penetrating and determined candour; the wild-hawk look still there, 'untamable, untranslatable,' yet with that wonderful tenderness at bottom."

The next day Walt came over, at noon, to Crowell's hotel, where I was staying; we dined and went to Fairmount Park in the afternoon. Talked a little about social questions. W.: "I believe, like Carlyle, in *men;* I think that notwithstanding all set-offs the great capitalists and masters of private enterprise have, in America at least, been useful.

I have myself had all along a tender feeling for Co-operation, but for that doubt whether a committee or an elected person could or would do the work." As to England, he seemed to think that emigration would relieve it, and he looked upon the law and custom of *entail* as the "hard-pan underlying your social institutions." "I like and welcome all agitation, even the fiercest, but like Carlyle have little belief in reform talk. Society, like a person in middle life, is *set*, and you have to make the best of it. I am, I hope, a bit of a reformer myself. Yes, we must *grow* generous, ungrasping masters of industry; absurd as the idea would seem to most now-a-days, I believe that is the upshot of what is going on. The creation of a large, independent, democratic class of small owners is the main thing—though it is never once mentioned by our economists and politicians.

I am satisfied that for America Free Trade and open admission of all foreigners is an integral part of its theory; the future of the world is one of open communication and solidarity of all races; and if that problem cannot be solved in America it cannot be solved anywhere."

We drove to Fairmount Park in a 'bus, walked a little, sat at the refreshment tables, and listened to the band—Walt absorbed and quiet for the most part, recognised by a few among the well-dressed crowd, but seeming to hold himself aloof with almost an air of *hauteur*—looking fine withal in his grey suit and with grey uncovered head, tho' perhaps a little weary. He asked me somewhat about my life and doings at home.

The following evening I stayed to supper with Whitman in the little kitchen of his home, in company with Mr. and Mrs. Lay. They seemed homely decent people, rather dull and quiet. Walt, who was dressed just in shirt and trousers—for the weather was hot—kept things going. Afterwards we sat in the front room with Folger McKinsey, a young Philadelphian of literary leanings, who had come in. Walt talked about Shakespeare, the Bacon theory, the greatness of the historical plays, the "dragon-rancours" of the barons, King Lear, &c. "I will not be positive about Bacon's connection with the plays, but I am satisfied that behind the historical Shakespeare there is another mind, guiding, and far, far reaching, giving weight and permanent value to what would otherwise have been only two plays a year written for a witty, alert, jocose audience—chiefly of young gallants."

The conversation turned somehow on death. W.: "It is in reality a very different affair from the romantic stage view of it; deathbed speeches and 'scenes' are of the rarest occurrence. I have witnessed hundreds of deaths, and as a rule it seems just a matter of course—like having your breakfast, or any other event of the day, and met with indifference at the last, and with apathy, or unconsciousness."

After an hour or two we went out and walked a little through the Camden streets—Walt, as usual, with plentiful greetings to passers-by. He would insist on our coming into a shop and having some refreshment, and then a few minutes later at the corner of a street, left us, I remember, with that queer brusque manner of his which so often offended his friends—just coldly saying "Ta-ta," and going off as if he didn't care if he never saw us again!

The next morning (June 30) was my last visit to Whitman; we had a long and intimate conversation. He was very friendly and affectionate, and sat by the open window downstairs enjoying the wafts of fragrant air, while he talked about "Leaves of Grass." "What lies behind 'Leaves of Grass' is something that few, very few, only one here and there, perhaps oftenest women, are at all in a position to seize. It lies behind almost every line; but concealed, studiedly concealed; some passages left purposely obscure. There is something in my nature *furtive* like an old hen! You see a hen wandering up and down a hedgerow, looking apparently quite unconcerned, but presently she finds a concealed spot, and furtively lays an egg, and comes away as though nothing had happened! That is how I felt in writing 'Leaves of Grass.' Sloane Kennedy calls me 'artful'—which about hits the mark. I think there are truths which it is necessary to envelop or wrap up." I replied that all through history the old mysteries, or whatever they may have been called, had been held back; and added that probably we had something yet to learn from India in these matters. W.: "I do not myself think there is anything more to come from that source; we must rather look to modern science to open the way. Time alone can absolutely test my poems or any one's. Personally, I think that the 'something' is more present in some of my small later poems than in the 'Song of Myself.'"

This was the last I saw of Whitman. I left him sitting there by the window in his downstairs room, close to the street and the passers-by—his clear eye undimmed by age, his rugged, loving nature unaltered; though there was a certain grave weariness in his otherwise majestic presence, which gives one a touch of sadness when one thinks that he had still nearly eight years to pass of increasing physical disablement and of continually diminishing vitality, culminating at last in serious bodily misery and wretchedness, before death might relieve him of the burden of the flesh.

It seems strange at first that Whitman's death should have been of such a lingering character—three months, from Christmas 1891, to near the end of the following March, in a dying state nearly all the time, with much restlessness, sleeplessness, misery, and even pain at times. But in some ways this was in consonance with his physical temperament—his extraordinarily voluminous hold on life, all phases of it, his extreme tenacity, his strong implication in the life of the body and the senses, his affectionate and unceasing love towards his friends, and his marked and obdurate egoism—all things which held him to life, and needed a long process of disentanglement, fibre by fibre as it were, before he could be released.

Volume—voluminousness—was one of Walt's most notable features. Physically it was so—as witness his ample proportions, his keen and well-furnished senses; mentally the same—a mind well stocked, interested in every subject, balancing, weighing, comparing, slow-moving, but never retracing its steps; emotionally and by temperament the same, with an immense range of emotion, and volume of feeling when roused, but slow, deliberate, cautious, lethargic, and at times even lumpishly immovable. This voluminousness is the key to his literary style, which at its best is magnificent—thought after thought culled from every side and department of life, ranged in successive line and phrase, marshalled and held in suspense as it were in huge array, till at last they are hurled upon the reader in one mass and with overwhelming power; but which style at its worst is cumbersome and disjointed. It is this voluminousness which goes with the whole florid full emotional nature of the man, fond of materials and plenty of materials, not especially careful of order or arrangement, not too studiedly clear or concise in thought and expression, but always ample and inclusive.

Another main point in Whitman's character is, I think, best expressed by the word "cussedness." I have touched on it once or twice: the contrary moods, the spirit of refusal, the wilfulness, which by their at times necessary opposition and antagonism to his ample and loving humanity formed, I believe, a great tragic element in his nature—and possibly prevented him ever being quite what is called "happy in love affairs." He celebrates in his poems the fluid, all-solvent disposition, but often was himself less the river than the rock. In these moods, fixed, silent, and unquestionable, he was a thing you might try your strength upon, but which you were not likely to move!

In the slow downward slope of his head from back to front, and in the lines of his eye and brow, tenacity was written; it looked out upon you from the small, well-defined pupil set under its long, curtain-like lid; and there was at times in his face, as I have said, the look as of a precipice, sheer, with breakneck ledges. One can imagine how this portion of his character, at any rate in his younger days, must have conflicted with his equally innate and imperious craving for human love and fellowship, and what suffering the conflict must have brought to him at times. R. W. Emerson said to me once (1877) of Whitman that when he came to know him he found him "a wayward, fanciful man."[1] This was not probably meant to be a complete account of the man, yet it indicates Emerson's perception of certain characteristics in him. In later

[1] See *infra*, p. 166.

years the large, equable human heart asserted itself more and more, and nothing could be more beautiful than the tolerance towards old and young of all sorts which he exhibited; while the waywardness became refined into something majestic. I remember old Mr. Pearsall Smith, of Philadelphia, who knew Whitman very well, saying that one of the things which impressed him most about Walt was his "magnificent No!"—how sometimes when invited out, or asked to do anything which he did not care to do, there would roll forth—unqualified by any thanks, or explanation, or excuse—the simple negative, with a great round O, and yet, as a rule, with a large sunny amiability which made offence impossible.

I have two portraits—photographs—which I am fond of comparing with each other. One is of Whitman, taken in 1890; the other, taken at about the same time and at the same age (seventy years), is of an Indian Gnani or seer. Both are faces of the highest interest and import; but how different! That of Whitman deeply lined, bearing the marks of life-long passion and emotion, aggressive and determined, yet wistful and tender, full of suffering and full of love, indicating serenity, yet markedly turbid and clouded, ample in brow and frame and flowing hair, as of one touching and mingling with humanity at all points — withal of a wonderful majesty and grandeur, as of the great rocks (to return always to that simile) whose summits pierce at last the highest domain.

The other portrait, of a man equally aged, shows scarcely a line on the face; you might think for that and for the lithe, active form that he was not more than forty years old; a brow absolutely calm and unruffled, gracious, expressive lips, well-formed features, and eyes—the dominant characteristic of his countenance—dark and intense, and illuminated by the vision of the seer. In this face you discern command, control, gentleness, and the most absolute inward unity, serenity, and peace; no wandering emotions or passions flit across the crystal mirror of the soul; self-hood in any but the highest sense has vanished—the self has, as it were, returned to its birthplace—leaving behind the most childlike, single-hearted, uncensorious, fearless character imaginable.

Yet just here one seems to miss something in the last character—the touch of human and earthly entanglement. Here is not exactly the great loving heart which goes a few steps on the way with every child of man; here is not the ample-domed brow which tackles each new problem of life and science. Notwithstanding evident signs of culture and experience in the past, notwithstanding vast power of concentration in any given matter or affair when necessary, the face shows that heart and intellect have become quiescent, that interest in the actual has passed or is passing away.

Whitman's immense moody and emotional temperament—he calls it "turbulent" himself—forms a factor of his character and writings, which has perhaps not been sufficiently considered—especially by some of his admirers, who, as so often happens, are more concerned to present an ideal personality than a real portrait. There are indeed some of his biographers who are at pains to explain that many of his expressions of sympathy and participation in the weaknesses and sins of humanity are to be taken as theoretical or allegorical expressions, having by no means a personal interpretation. Yet surely this is to take the clay out of the brick, the marble out of the statue. While it is obvious that no man could have in one lifetime run through *all* the experiences mentioned in "Leaves of Grass," the whole point of the matter is that the author actually finds in himself the capability of these experiences, and quite personally identifies himself with them. It is, in fact, just these earth-entanglements, in a character so cosmic in its range as his, which are of special import as giving direction and effect to his individuality and to his work. Not only is it clear that without his voluminous enfoldment in the earth-life—the Nessus-shirt of Hercules—he could not well have performed the mighty works that he did; but it is difficult to see how, without some of that obduracy and egotism of his, he could have held his own against the great surge of obloquy and ridicule which covered his first appearance on the field of literature. Whitman saw (somewhere within himself) the typical man of a new era; and he gave himself to the utterance of what he saw. It stood in the most glaring and irremediable contrast to the genteel ideal of the civilisation around him. Alone, he had to confront the whole of modern society. Now then, if ever, strength was needed. Now then tenacity, obstinacy, wilfulness; they had to be made the most of. If they were faults they were such as could ill be spared. His was perhaps the most deliberately daring advance ever made in literature; and it is difficult to believe that it could have been made except by one in whom the rocky elements of character were abundantly present. "Leaves of Grass" itself has this quality of undeniable "thereness"; and when the critics have had their say and expended all their shafts upon it, it still remains solid and untouched—like the earth, which survives all the theories of the geologists and surrenders itself to none.

There is a third point. In many ways Whitman marks a stage of human evolution not yet reached, and hardly suspected, by humanity at large; but in no respect is this more true than in respect of his capacity of Love. If you consider Whitman's life you will see that Love ruled it, that he gave his life for love. There were other motives no doubt, but this one ultimately dominated them all. It permeates like a flame his entire writings; it took him to the battlefield and the hospitals in succour of the wounded soldiers; it led him (before the war) deep into the life and comradeship of the people—all phases; after the war it united him in bonds of tender and life-long friendship with many,[1] both men and women; it

[1] See his Letters to Pete Doyle, published under the title "Calamus," by Small, Maynard & Co., Boston, U.S.A.

surrounded his death-bed with devotion, and brought thousands to his funeral. For it he gave away his possessions and the material means of life, he gave his prospects of professional success, he gave health, fame—all that a man can give—and accepted illness and obscurity, and oftentimes long and painful loneliness and betrayal even of love itself.[1]

He was a man in whom the power of

---

[1] See that remarkable poem printed in the 1860 edition of "Leaves of Grass" (p. 355), but afterwards omitted, perhaps as being too personal:—

"Hours continuing long, sore and heavy-hearted,
Hours of the dusk, when I withdraw to a lonesome and unfrequented spot, seating myself, leaning my face in my hands;
Hours sleepless, deep in the night, when I go forth, speeding swiftly the country roads, or through the city streets, or pacing miles and miles, stifling plaintive cries;
Hours discouraged, distracted—for the one I cannot content myself without, soon I saw him content himself without me;
Hours when I am forgotten, (O weeks and months are passing, but I believe I am never to forget!)

love was developed to an extraordinary degree. Yet (thanks to him) this was no attenuated or merely spiritual love, but was a large and generous passion, spiritual and emotional of course, but well rooted in the physical and sexual also. In him the various sides and manifestations of the passion were so blent, that instead of weakening they recognised and reinforced each other; and, coming

---

Sullen and suffering hours! (I am ashamed—but it is useless—I am what I am;)
Hours of my torment—I wonder if other men ever have the like, out of the like feelings?
Is there even one like me—distracted—his friend, his lover, lost to him?
Is he too as I am now? Does he still rise in the morning, dejected, thinking who is lost to him? and at night, awaking, think who is lost?
Does he too harbor his friendship silent and endless? harbor his anguish and passion?
Does some stray reminder, or the casual mention of a name, bring the fit back upon him, taciturn and deprest?
Does he see himself reflected in me? In these hours does he see the face of his hours reflected?"

into touch with humanity, as he did with a kind of careless equalness from all these sides; piercing through the layers and folds of caste, through differences of race, climate, character, occupation; despising distances of space and time; he drew men and women of the most varied nature and habits to himself, saved them from their own little selves—from their own little virtues and vices—and united them in the solidarity of humanity, by their common attachment to him. "Leaves of Grass" is the meeting-ground of the human race. There every nationality, every creed, every trade, every atom of humanity is represented, and all are fused in the great loving soul that overbroods them.

If it seems difficult to reconcile this great and abounding charity of Whitman with his strong egotism, it is perhaps not needful to reconcile them. They may have been two necessarily opposite poles of his nature. At any rate to assert this love—physical, sexual, emotional, spiritual—extending to all races, castes, to the most despised and degraded, to the near home and far off, to the virtuous and to the criminal, to men as well as to women, to the animals even—in all its phases and utterances; and to assert this egoism, plainly, unblushingly, in all its forms—confidence, pride, self-esteem, desire, and delight in all the natural powers and appetites—Whitman deliberately set himself. In doing so he (necessarily) upset all former and formal moralities, and exposed himself to the fiercest opposition; but some day—when it has come to be recognised that the medium in which the true *ego*, the soul, lives and moves is neither gain nor fame, nor duty nor denial, but indeed love and love alone—it will be seen that

"Leaves of Grass" is, perhaps of all books ever written, the most natural and nobly inevitable.

A fourth point which I will venture to touch on in this estimate of Whitman—perhaps the most vital of all, but impossible to be adequately seized or expressed—is what may be called his 'illumination.' "Leaves of Grass," of course, would not have been written without it; it runs behind every page—"the vision and the faculty divine." This perception in the universal, this power of seeing things apart from the mundane self, and independent of their relation to that self, appears to be a kind of transcendent faculty in man; which occasionally manifests itself, and which brings him—it may perhaps be said—into relation with another order of existence. Indeed the strangeness of the sensation, and the intoxication of this vision, appears sometimes to be so great that—as in the case of the blinding glare at the mouth of Plato's cavern ("Republic," bk. vii.) —the beholder after witnessing it is unhinged for ordinary life, and can neither see the things of the world in their accustomed light, nor describe clearly what else it is that he has seen. This it is, no doubt, that constitutes the partial 'mania' of the poet (Plato's "Phædrus"), and which accounts also for the fact that many people of mystical tendency, after a momentary illumination of the kind, relapse into a sort of drivel for the rest of their natural lives—circling always round something which they have neither clearly apprehended nor can conclusively forget —but out of the memory of which they hatch systems and 'revelations' and dogmas without end. And indeed, if we suppose, with Dr. Bucke, that the faculty is one that is gradually evolving in human nature, there can be nothing more likely than that its first exercise should be accompanied by much doubt and illusion and disturbance of the intelligence generally, and even of the moral nature.

In the case of Whitman, however, the immense sanity of his intelligence and his immense grasp of the actual world prevented any serious dislocation of the kind; and, though the mania and intoxication are at times almost terrific (as in the 'Song of Myself'), he never loses his hold on actual facts, but manages at last to draw them in a great web over himself, and to show the whole world transparent with the illumination within.

This faculty of perception in the universal must not be looked upon as a mere intellectual discrimination of certain facts or objects; it is rather, I take it, a conscious *identity* with the object ("I *am* the mash'd fireman with breastbone broken"); in which consciousness the emotional and sensational elements are fused with the intellectual, just as they are in the consciousness of one's own existence and actions. It is a universal light which falls as it were on the interior side of all objects, enabling the person that moves along it to penetrate to their very essence and to perceive their abiding relation to each other. And the faculty begins to develop itself normally in those (as one would expect) whose emotional and intellectual nature is becoming universal. When sympathy and intelligence on the ordinary plane have grown so far as to bring the man into free and unprejudiced relation with almost every phase of existence, then this new perception dawns upon him; the scales fall from the eyes which have always before seen by the light of self, and he sees by the light "which never was on sea or land." "Willst du ins Unendliche schreiten, geh' nur im Endlichen nach allen Seiten," says Goethe; not that the mere travelling through the finite of itself brings one to the 'infinite,' but that it prepares the human being as it were for his translation into it, when the time comes.

With Whitman it would seem that he had travelled along the finite in pretty well every direction, when, about the age of thirty-five or thirty-six, or near that time, this new order of consciousness, and of being, opened out upon him. Instead of upsetting his broadly-based voluminous nature, it immediately established that nature, forming the nucleus to its endless ramifications, and the key and reconcilement of its contrary moods. His luxuriant turbulent emotional passional self acknowledged instantly its Lord in the universal ("swiftly arose and spread around me the peace and the knowledge that pass all the argument of the earth"); and became dedicated to that service thenceforward; and all the conflicting elements of his own nature and of general nature were seen—as they must be in such a case—to have their justification and their use. "The moth and the fish-eggs are in place."

With Whitman the new perception was eminently sane and undistorted. It is probable indeed that never in historical times has the cosmic intuition found a fuller and more complete utterance; for it was not dwindled away into any mere thin and other-worldly ecstasy, denying in a kind of spiritual excess the claims of the body and the intellect, but was blent and harmonised, in fiery union, with the very widest practical experiences and the inferences of a singularly rich nature. For the first time in history do we hear the voice of a prophet who really *knows* and really *accepts* the whole range of human life.

The last twenty-five of Whitman's years were overshadowed by the clouds of partial and intermittent paralysis. From the miracle of health and strength which he had been before the war, it was his destiny to come near to being a chronic invalid. Unfitted for active life, unfitted even for much literary work, he quietly accepted his lot; and being unable to express his message in any more resounding way, was content to fashion the commonplaces of his daily life to its utterance; and no one, I think, could witness the dignity and simple beauty of this later life without feeling that here, in its way, was a poem as pregnant as "Leaves of Grass." Gentle and humane in manners, the rocky bases of his nature—if such had been conspicuous before—now covered with tender herbage and flowers, making the most of small details, fond of children, and with a pleasant cheery word for all, letting life come and go with large equanimity, he was a man whom the simplest could approach without effort, and who was loved by hundreds who never read a word of his writing. If he had a preference, it was for the "common people." The unconscious, uncultured, natural types pleased him best, and he would make an effort to approach them. The others he allowed to approach him.

NOTES AND APPRECIATIONS

Allen & Co. Sc.

Walt Whitman

at the age of 53

WHITMAN AS PROPHET

DR. R. MAURICE BUCKE, in his "Memories of Walt Whitman,"[1] speaking of the years 1853–55, and of the inception of "Leaves of Grass," says, "A very few years before these dates we find Walt Whitman writing tales, essays, sketches, and even poems, which are in no way distinguishable from that 'mighty tide of ditch water' which Carlyle tells us flows day by day from the power-presses of civilisation. All at once he writes the greatest book of a great century. Where did he get the stuff to

[1] "Walt Whitman Fellowship Papers" (Philadelphia, 1894), p. 42.

put in it? How did he get it all in a minute, as it were? Or, if it was in him before, why did it not show itself? My memories of Walt Whitman include many talks, in which I did my best to obtain light upon these and related problems. Generally, he would pass over the subject with a half-answer or a return question; at other times he would be more explicit, as he was one day in the summer of 1886, when he said—'*Leaves of Grass* was there, though unformed, all the time, in whatever answers as the laboratory of the mind. I was more or less conscious of it, and thought often of taking action in that direction. But, you can understand, there was much to deter—that until the impulse to move had become very strong, nothing would be done. I could clearly see that such an enterprise would meet with little favor—at all events at first—that it would be hooted at (as it was) and perhaps hooted down. The *Democratic Review* essays and tales came from the surface of the mind, and had no connection with what lay below—a great deal of which indeed was below consciousness. At last came the time when the concealed growth had to come to light, and the first edition of *Leaves of Grass* was written and published.'"

This phrase, "the concealed growth had to come to light," thus preserved for us by Dr. Bucke, helps much towards the appreciation of the prophetic and unexpected character of "Leaves of Grass." We do not of course understand why out of green foliage and branches a sudden and unexpected blossom—yet evidently long prepared in the heart of the plant—should appear; nor do we understand why, often amid quite unpromising foliage of the human mind, a great work of art or prophecy arises; yet we seem to see that the processes are very similar. A centre of growth, hitherto unnoticed, long hidden, has come to light.

Prophecy at all times has this inevitable spontaneous character, as of something arising from below the ordinary consciousness, which just for the very reason that it so arises cannot be deliberately quenched or stopped — something almost inarticulate, hardly gaining the sphere of definition; irrational, and out of joint with accepted things; subversive, inconvenient, contrary; annunciative of a new order. The prophets are stoned; for they are obviously liars and iconoclasts. They are charged with inconsistency, and, poor things! they cannot deny the charge. They cannot help themselves. The flower unfolding out of its own roots cannot unfold other than it does.

By many such marks Whitman's work

shows a prophetic character. And while he does not claim to deliver a new Gospel, he seems to claim to take his place in the line of those who have handed down a world-old treasure of redemption for mankind. In his poem, "To Him that was Crucified,"[1] he says:—

"My spirit to yours, dear brother,
Do not mind because many sounding your name do not understand you,
I do not sound your name, but I understand you,
I specify you with joy, O my comrade, to salute you, and to salute those that are with you, before and since, and those to come also,
That we all labor together transmitting *the same charge and succession*,
We few equals, indifferent of lands, indifferent of times,
We, enclosers of all continents, all castes, allowers of all theologies,
Compassionaters, perceivers, rapport of men,
We walk silent among disputes and assertions, but reject not the disputers nor anything that is asserted,

[1] "Leaves of Grass," p. 298.

We hear the bawling and the din, we are reach'd at by divisions, jealousies, recriminations on every side,
They close peremptorily on us to surround us, my comrade,
Yet we walk unheld, free, the whole earth over, journeying up and down till we make our ineffaceable mark upon time and the diverse eras,
Till we saturate time and eras, that the men and women of races, ages to come, may prove brethren and lovers as we are."

It will be noticed that in this great poem he speaks not merely as a successor of him that was crucified, but as a continuer of some world-wide and agelong tradition. And in truth we cannot doubt that the root of it all *has* been known and realised since the farthest history; the charge and succession have certainly descended out of dim obscurity from the earliest times. How much exactly Walt Whitman may have known of the Vedic and other early writings is doubtful; but that he had read here and there among them, quite enough to gain an insight into the heart of them, and to know that his message was continuous with theirs, is quite certain. "These are really the thoughts of men in all ages and lands, they are not original with me." In the Vedic scriptures, and, in lineal succession from these, in the Buddhist and Platonist and Christian writings, in the Taoists of China, the Mystics of Egypt, the Sufis of Persia, the root is to be found—and is clearly distinguishable—the very same from which "Leaves of Grass" has sprung. [It would be too long at present, by quotations from all these writings, to attempt to prove this; but in an Appendix to this paper I have, in very imperfect fashion, dotted in a number of parallel passages from them and from "Leaves of Grass," and these may serve to illustrate what I mean.] A glance at these ancient and modern utterances assures us that all down history the same loving universal spirit has looked out, making its voice heard from time to time, harmonising the diverse eras, enclosing continents, castes, and theologies. The same charge and succession has passed on, and Whitman voices and transmits it in his turn.

Yet of course there are differences. We cannot say that Whitman is more subtle, more penetrating, more profound than many of those who have gone before. It would be hard to imagine anything more subtle and profound than passages in the Upanishads. But in one respect he is certainly unique among the prophets, and that is in the universality and breadth of his appeal. He seems to *liberate* the good tidings and give it a democratic scope and world-wide application unknown in the elder prophets, even in the sayings of Buddha.

The difficulty with the earlier prophets no doubt was that around them limitations existed on every hand. Races, peoples, religions, were sharply divided from each other. In the early world exclusiveness was indispensable. The peoples and nations could not have grown up if each had not believed that its own customs, morals, religion, race, &c., were infinitely superior to those of the others. Exclusiveness and war were the nurses of growing humanity's powers—of comradeship, organised life, community of sentiment, courage, self-sacrifice, and all the early virtues. Problems of social life and character, which could never have been solved in a general ocean of mankind, were easy to define and determine in small communities. Ignorance and prejudice were necessary fences between one state or system of society and another. And however great certain individual teachers may have been in the past—however generous and wide their real outlook on life, they still could only act and speak subject to the very definite limitations prevailing around them.[1] The Joels, Jeremiahs, Mohammeds, Carlyles, —stung no doubt by incontrollable impulse to blaze forth that which was in them — have delivered their special messages: have called the people of their time to gather themselves round some new centre of life and inspiration, moral or religious or racial; and in doing so have anathematised every other code of morals or form of religion, called all outside people Gentiles or Barbarians, and put them to the sword. They have done work priceless in their

[1] We have to remember, too, that their sayings have come down to us only through priestly, local, racial media. There is not a sacred book that has not been tampered with, and its teaching distorted in the direction of narrowing and exclusiveness.

time and locality, insisting on and compelling each some certain and necessary step in human progress; and having done so, they have gone their way and been superseded, because their message was only a part-message. Only a few have not been superseded. Teachers like the Buddha, Jesus of Nazareth, St. Francis, and the Syrian Bâb,[1] belong to no race or nationality; if they press the claims of religion or morality, it is with so little insistence on any particular scheme or code, that their net may be said to be spread to catch all humanity. They are accepters rather than deniers; they represent the prophetic gift in its deepest and most inclusive utterance; and it is difficult to think of them as becoming antiquated or out of date.

Yet—though it would not be acceptable

[1] See "Abbas Effendi," a study of the religion of the Babis, by M. H. Phelps (Putnams, 1903).

or desirable to make comparisons of greatness—we may say that even among these Whitman was (with the exception perhaps of the Bâb) unique in the realisation of the world-wide and universal character of his message. The others had messages of world-wide import to deliver, though perhaps they hardly knew this at the time; but Whitman realised from the first that this universality was the very key and centre of his utterance, and set himself deliberately to emphasise it. Many things conspired, with him, to this result—the girdling of the earth in his time, and the extraordinary developments of locomotion and intercommunication which were bringing together East and West, and all races and classes, creeds and customs, into close touch and acknowledgment of each other. The peoples were being compelled to see that none of them has a monopoly of excellence or defect, but that all illustrate, in their various ways, forms of necessary life. The Press, the Locomotive, the Wire, were pushing more and more insistently to this conclusion. The fences were breaking down; a new Era was shaping; and Whitman himself, by a nature and temperament of extraordinary balance and fulness, physical, mental, and moral ("I can resist anything better than my own diversity"), was fitted to respond to it all—to swim in this ocean of humanity as in a sea.

[Yet even so, and allowing for the occasioning causes, it must be said that his utterance, in its dæmonic reach and sweep, is somewhat staggering! Through "Leaves of Grass" pours a torrent of trades, classes, characters, occupations, races, nations, morals, manners, incidents, opinions — things generally accounted beautiful, and things unbeautiful, things good or evil, proper or improper—in huge indifference, all apparently accepted on an equality, dismissed on an equality. It is, to certain folk, most confusing, and at times even revolting and terrifying.]

Of this new Era, with all its splendours and terrors, Walt Whitman may be said to be the prophet. Through the "barbaric yawp" and seeming-random medley of his verse—inarticulate enough at times in its very endeavour to include and accept every phase and feature of human life—break out the deep-rolling organ-tones of Creation's primal music. We hear the same agelong theme and symphony of all historic time, gaining, through whatever imperfections, a larger freer expression by virtue of its so much more extended key-board and orchestra, by virtue of its discords and sequences more daring than ever used in literature before.

And the Theme? Whitman has defined it very directly at the first outset of his poems:—

> "One's Self I sing, a simple separate person,
> Yet utter the word Democratic, the word En-Masse."

The Self, individual and separate, yet conjoined and continuous throughout Creation's mass—that is the theme which undoubtedly runs through the whole of his poems and prophetic utterances. And it is the theme of the eldest Upanishads of the Vedic sages. It is the theme which has come down through the ages—variously balanced, with now somewhat more insistence on one aspect, now somewhat more on another; variously expressed and illustrated, in poetical, religious, or philosophical form; variously coloured, confined, or conventionalised by race and tradition; but inevitably gaining in the long-run in freedom and fulness of utterance. In Whitman it breaks out almost unconsciously—certainly less as the result of any intellectual process or argument than by force of an irresistible impulse—into a strange torrential pæan of identity. Everything, the whole earth, all its shows, men and women, sinners and saints, the stars, insects, solar systems —all beings are envisaged in order to be identified with the One; they are accorded each their unique unapproachable character and perfection, only to be embraced :—

> "We make our ineffaceable mark upon time and the diverse eras,
> Till we saturate time and eras, that the men and women of races, ages to come, may prove brethren and lovers as we are."

So in Whitman all the purblind morals and moonlight ideals of the past are, whether directly or by implication, broken up (hence storm and terror to many) and led back to their most central motive, the world-old revelation of the Self, eternal and inseparate.

> "I ascend from the moon, I ascend from the night,
> I perceive that the ghastly glimmer is noonday sunbeams reflected,
> And debouch to the steady and central from the offspring great or small."

Always the inward, the enduring, the central, the vital, is acknowledged and honoured; the external, the temporary, the unessential thrown off. Underneath all morals, manners, races, titles, classes, the original human soul and its affections, greater than all. Underneath clothing, costume, ranks, trades, and occupations, the bodily form, its needs and physiology. Underneath all art and social life, sex and fraternity. Greater than all houses, temples, galleries, and museums, the life of the open air and its lessons. In such simple elementary things as these—in the universal human soul, rediscovering itself in all forms, in the healthy and beautiful human body, in sex and fraternity, in the life with the earth and the open air, Whitman sees the root out of which future humanity will spring (as it has sprung in the past): out of which a society of proud, strong, free individuals, who shall also be brethren and lovers, may easily and naturally arise:—

> "Now if a thousand perfect men were to appear it would not amaze me,
> Now if a thousand beautiful forms of women appear'd it would not astonish me."

We may indeed say that, with the signal appearance of "Leaves of Grass," the hour has struck for mankind of liberation, of emancipation, from mere outer rules and limitations; the hour for the reference of all life, irrespective of colour, creeds, and principles, to its central essence.

It may be, for reasons already hinted, an hour of danger. Not a few, accustomed only to walk by well-worn paths and formulæ, will lose their way. "Take warning! He traveling with me needs the best blood, thews, endurance." But it is an hour which must needs come; and it opens for humanity on an era of unexampled glory.

And here a word about Individuals. It will be recognised by all readers of Whitman that his insistence on the permanence, the immortality, the supreme life of the Individual, is a most marked feature of his teaching. "The sum of all known reverence I add up in you whoever you are." "Yourself! yourself! yourself for ever and ever!" "I sing the songs of the glory of none, not God, sooner than I sing the songs of the glory of you." For Whitman every Self in its essence is individual, eternal, perfect, accruing to itself alone: "I swear I think now that everything without exception has an eternal soul!"

> "Each man to himself and each woman to herself is the word of the past and present, and the true word of immortality;
> No one can acquire for another—not one;
> No one can grow for another—not one."

And yet (strange paradox!) all are One.

> "Have you thought there could be but a single Supreme?
> There can be any number of Supremes—one does not countervail another any more than one eyesight countervails another, or one life countervails another."

Each is a simple separate person, and yet *en-masse* with the rest. I think we may say that no former teacher has quite dared to give this side of the truth as Whitman has done, nor given it with so free and so splendid an expression.

Thus it may seem that if in the matter of pure philosophical statement Whitman does not stand out in the great charge and succession so strongly as some of his predecessors, yet in two respects at least his work is unique: namely, in the universality and determination of his appeal to, and brotherhood with, all creation, and in his insistence on the root-existence of every Individual from everlasting to everlasting — his protest, in fact (though quite indirect), against a mere doctrine of absorption in the Universal.

One other point I should like to note —and it goes with the preceding remarks —namely, Whitman's extraordinary *concreteness*, and his consistent and set avoidance of abstract doctrine in the highest regions of thought. "I swear I see what is better than to tell the best, it is always to leave the best untold." This avoidance is so subtle and determined that many readers are deceived by it into not perceiving "beautiful things well envelop'd," and into thinking Whitman himself did not perceive them. The reason of it is clear. Whitman refused to address himself to the Brain alone. He saw that with regard to the highest truths it is useless to try to seize or impart them that way. They must be *felt* as well as thought. To try to *think* them alone, as one would prove a syllogism, is a kind of blasphemy. And to create the feeling, the direct awareness and consciousness of the highest facts, one must proceed in another way; one must use the method of Indirection—the method of Life and Time and the Earth, as well as of all great Art and Literature—the appeal through sense and all concrete experience, penetrating, far-reaching, cumulative in its power, till it wake the profoundest deeps of the soul. Through Whitman's pages all the shows of the Earth, and myriads of concrete images, surge and break upon the sensitive mind-surface of the reader—who in many cases as little understands or suspects what their meaning and intention is, as every child of Man suspects the meaning of the winds and waters that play around him as he walks. Nevertheless they convince by their presence. They wake and build up new ranges of feeling in him. They filter and fibre his blood. And it is this concreteness, this power of indirect appeal, which constitute Whitman great among the Poets—even as his unrivalled knowledge of the actual world and of actual life, and his absolute *acceptance* of the same, give him so high a distinction among the Prophets.

APPENDIX TO WHITMAN AS PROPHET

(*See page* 77)

Passages from early prophetic writings[1]:—

"He, the Highest Person, who is awake in us while we are asleep, shaping one lovely sight after another; that indeed is the Bright, that is Brahman, that alone is called the Immortal." —*Katha Upanishad.*

"He is the one God, hidden in all beings, all

---

[1] Compare the following from "Leaves of Grass":—

"O Thou transcendent,
Nameless, the fibre and the breath,
Light of the light, shedding forth universes . . .
Swiftly I shrivel at the thought of God,
At Nature and its wonders, Time and Space and Death,
But that I, turning, call to thee O soul, thou actual Me,
And lo! thou gently masterest the orbs,
Thou matest Time, smilest content at Death,
And fillest, swellest full the vastnesses of Space."
(p. 321.)

pervading, the Self within all beings, watching over all works, dwelling in all beings, the witness, the Perceiver, the only one, free from qualities."—*Svetasvatara Upanishad.*

"The sun does not shine [show] there, nor the moon and the stars, nor these lightnings, and much less this fire. When he shines, everything shines after him; by his light all this [world] is lightened."—*Svetasvatara Upanishad.*

"As rain water that has fallen on a mountain ridge runs down on all sides, thus does he who sees a difference between qualities run after them on all sides.

"Light rare untellable, lighting the very light,
Beyond all signs, descriptions, languages." (p. 324.)

"Whoever you are! you are he or she for whom the earth is solid and liquid;
You are he or she for whom the sun and moon hang in the sky." (p. 178.)

"I celebrate Myself,
And what I assume, you shall also assume." (p. 29.)

"Apart from the pulling and hauling stands what I am,
Stands amused, complacent, compassionating, idle, unitary,
Both in and out of the game, and watching and wondering at it." (p. 32.)

"Evil propels me, and reform of evil propels me,
I stand indifferent." (p. 46.)

"As pure water poured into pure water remains the same, thus, O Gautama, is the Self of a thinker who knows."—*Katha Upanishad.*

"By the serenity of his thoughts a man blots out all actions, whether good or bad. Dwelling within the Self with serene thoughts he obtains imperishable happiness."—*Maitrayana-Brahmana Upanishad.*

"And he who beholds all beings in the Self, and the Self in all beings, he never turns away from it.

"When to a man who understands, the Self has become all things, what sorrow, what trouble, can there be to him who once beheld that unity?"—*Vagasaneyi-Samhita Upanishad.*

The Blessed one [Buddha] said to Ananda: "Both the ocean and my doctrine become

---

"What is called good is perfect, and what is called bad is just as perfect." (p. 337.)

"Swiftly arose and spread around me the peace and knowledge that pass all the argument of the earth." (p. 32.)

"No array of terms can say how much I am at peace about God and about death." (p 76.)

"My spirit has pass'd in compassion and determination around the whole earth.
I have look'd for equals and lovers, and found them ready for me in all lands." (p. 120.)

gradually deeper. Both preserve their identity under all changes. Both cast out dead bodies upon the dry land. As the great rivers, when falling into the main, lose their name and are thenceforth reckoned as the great ocean, so all the castes, having renounced their lineage and entered the Sangha [brotherhood], become brethren and are reckoned the sons of Shâkyamuni. The ocean is the goal of all streams and of the rain from the clouds, yet is it never overflowing and never emptied; so the dharma is embraced by many millions of people, yet it neither increases nor decreases. As the great ocean has only one taste, the taste of salt, so my doctrine has only one flavour, the flavour of emancipation. Both the ocean and the dharma

---

"Agonies are one of my changes of garments. I do not ask the wounded person how he feels, I myself become the wounded person." (p. 60.)

"I swear the earth shall surely be complete to him or her who shall be complete." (p. 179.)

"All parts away for the progress of souls,
All religion, all solid things, arts, governments—all that was or is apparent upon this globe, or any globe, falls into niches and corners before the procession of souls along the grand roads of the universe." (p. 127.)

are full of gems and pearls and jewels, and both afford a dwelling-place for mighty beings.

"My doctrine is pure, and it makes no discrimination between noble and ignoble, rich and poor. My doctrine is like unto water which cleanses all without distinction. My doctrine is like unto fire which consumes all things that exist between heaven and earth, great and small. My doctrine is like unto the heavens, for there is room in it, ample room, for the reception of all, for men and women, boys and girls, the powerful and the lowly."—*Mahâparinibbâna Suttanta*, iii. 22.

"He who believes that this spirit can kill," says Krishna to Arjuna, "and he who thinks that it can be killed, both of these are wrong in judgment. It neither kills, nor is killed. It is not born, nor dies at any time. It has had no origin, nor will it ever have an origin.

"As a man abandons worn-out clothes and takes other new ones, so does the soul quit

---

"Allons! whoever you are come travel with me!
Traveling with me you find what never tires." (p. 125.)

"This is the meal equally set, this the meat for natural hunger,
It is for the wicked just the same as the righteous; I make appointments with all." (p. 43.)

worn-out bodies, and enter other new ones. Weapons cannot cleave it. Fire cannot burn it, nor can water wet it, nor can wind dry it." —*Bhagavad Gita.*

"I am the same to all beings. I have neither foe nor friend. But those who worship me with devotion dwell in me and I also in them.

"He who discovers inaction in action, and action in inaction, is wise among mortals.

"The practiser of Yoga, whose spirit is purified, who has subdued himself and vanquished his senses, whose Self is the Self of all creatures, is not polluted even by action."—*Ibid.*

"I swear I think now that everything has an immortal soul!
I swear I think there is nothing but immortality." (p. 337.)

"Who, constructing the house of himself or herself, not for a day but for all time, sees races, eras, dates, generations,
The past, the future, dwelling there, like space, inseparable together." (p. 304.)

"I doubt not I have myself died ten thousand times before.
I receive now again of my many translations, from my avataras ascending, while others doubtless await me." (p. 382.)

"You can do nothing and be nothing but what I will infold you." (p. 66.)

"Tao as it exists in the world is like the great rivers and seas which receive the streams from the valleys.

"All pervading is the great Tao. It can be at once on the right hand and on the left. All things depend on it for life, and it rejects them not. Its task accomplished, it takes no credit. It loves and nourishes all things, but does not act as master. It is ever free from desire.

"We may call it small. All things return to it, yet it does not act as master. We may call it great.

"The whole world will flock to him who holds the mighty form of Tao. They will come and receive no hurt, but find rest, peace, and tranquillity."—*Sayings of Lao-tzu.*

"By non - action there is nothing which

"All truths wait in all things,
They neither hasten their own delivery nor resist it, . . .
The insignificant is as big to me as any." (p. 53.)

"I am possess'd!
Embody all presences outlaw'd or suffering." (p. 64.)

"I will toss a new gladness and roughness among them,
Whoever denies me it shall not trouble me,
Whoever accepts me he or she shall be blessed and shall bless me." (p. 123.)

cannot be done. Failure is the foundation of success, and the means by which it is achieved. Success is the lurking-place of failure; and who can tell when the turning-point will come?

"He who acts, destroys; he who grasps, loses. Therefore the sage does not act, and so does not destroy; he does not grasp, and so he does not lose.

"Only he who does nothing for his life's sake can truly be said to value his life.

"When the great Tao falls into disuse, benevolence and righteousness come into vogue. Cast off your holiness, rid yourself of your cleverness, and the people will benefit an hundredfold."—*Ibid.*

"I am the Way [Tao, the open Road], the Truth, and the Life.

"Woe unto you, Scribes and Pharisees, hypocrites! for ye shut up the kingdom of heaven against men: for ye neither go in yourselves, neither suffer ye them that are entering to go in.

"Vivas to those who have fail'd!" (p. 43.)

"What is providence is indivisible,
Declines to separate one part of life from every part, . . .
Knows that the young man who composedly peril'd his life and lost it has done exceedingly well for himself without doubt." (p. 291.)

Woe unto you, Scribes and Pharisees, hypocrites! for ye devour widows' houses, and for a pretence make long prayers: therefore ye shall receive the greater damnation.

"Come unto me, all ye that labour and are heavy laden, and I will give you rest. Take my yoke upon you, and learn of me; for I am meek and lowly in heart: and ye shall find rest unto your souls.

"For whosoever will save his life shall lose it; but whosoever shall lose his life for my sake and the good tidings, the same shall save it.

"And lo! I am with you alway, even unto the end of the world."—*Jesus in the Gospels.*

"Sleep—I and they keep guard all night;
Not doubt, not decease shall dare to lay finger upon you.
I have embraced you, and henceforth possess you to myself,
And when you rise in the morning you will find what I tell you is so." (p. 66.)

"Camerado, I give you my hand,
I give you my love more precious than money." (p. 129.)

"Toward you all, in America's name,
I raise high the perpendicular hand, I make the signal,
To remain after me in sight forever,
For all the haunts and homes of men." (p. 120.)

THE POETIC FORM OF "LEAVES OF GRASS"

OF all the tribes of specially *literary* people (one sometimes thinks), of the Popes, Drydens, Swinburnes, Paters, the Brownings or Tennysons even, not to mention hosts of lesser names—which of them, after all, as time goes on, and except for certain antiquarian interests and a few passages which represent the real unloading of the writers' hearts, will really be affectionately remembered or persistently read? A few pithy passages, of verse or tale, enshrining some vivid sharp experience—and for the rest what a deluge of words! The touch on actual life so thin, so poor, so ignorant. The society, yes, which animates itself round a Rape of a Lock, or discusses Broad Church questions over the walnuts and the wine, is there—but of the great world, what? A shade of sentiment or of thought, interesting enough, no doubt, and which may happen to be in vogue among a certain class—but of the great reaches of human passion and experience how much—or how little? Words, words, and fine-spun forms out of the thinnest basis of material! At every turn of the page gross misapprehensions and ignorance of the actual lives and conditions of life and heart of the thousands and millions and thousand-millions of the earth! How can these things hold any readers except those whose outlook is equally blinkered? The purely literary work has its interest, has its place; but its appeal is so limited.

With Whitman, the workman, the normal (or "average") man—for of course the man who deals with materials and wins his living from them *is* the normal man—comes, for the first time, in a deliberate and representative way, into literature. He comes, not as a man who abandons his former mode of life in order to seek a literary ideal, but as the master-workman who *stays where he is* and uses literary form for his own expression—and with the same directness and mastery that he uses towards life. Hence a new era of literature—a literature appealing to all who deal with life directly, and know what it is, a literature which will be read and lovingly absorbed by the millions as time goes on.

We may perhaps say that in every great artist there is something of the manner of the workman. In Michel Angelo, in

Beethoven, in Velasquez, in Pheidias, in Dante—a certain clearing for action, economy, directness, decisiveness. The good workman wants to make his work absolutely effective. That is his first thought. The great artist will not stop short of the most clear and perfect expression. He will do nothing to cloud it. In a note of Whitman's, for his own use, we find recommended as a rule for composition "the most translucid clearness without variation."[1] And every one must feel that the first and root-criterion of form is Expression. If the work conveys the meaning perfectly, then obviously any *change* of form (which necessarily must bring some change of meaning with it) will be a loss. Therefore, the expression being perfect, the form is also perfect. The two cannot be separated. We may

[1] "Notes and Fragments," left by Walt Whitman, and edited by R. M. Bucke (1899), p. 70.

analyse or examine the form in such a case—but to propose to alter it is mere foolishness. Read again the poem "To Him that was Crucified," quoted in the preceding paper, and realise the wonderful burden of thought and emotion conveyed, and then also realise that a single word displaced or altered anywhere in the poem would blur or diminish its total message and expression.

Is it possible indeed in these cases of perfect excellence, to stop and examine the form as a thing apart? I do not say that it is impossible; but it is surely very difficult. Are there not some pieces of music so beautiful, that though we try again and again while hearing them to analyse their form, we simply fail to do so? And are there not poems of which the mind refuses to count the syllables. Read, for example, the following from "Leaves of Grass":—

RECONCILIATION

Word over all, beautiful as the sky!
Beautiful that war and all its deeds of carnage must in time be utterly lost;
That the hands of the sisters Death and Night incessantly softly wash again, and ever again, this soil'd world.
For my enemy is dead, a man divine as myself is dead.
I look where he lies white-faced and still in the coffin—I draw near;
Bend down and touch lightly with my lips the white face in the coffin.

Here underneath, all the time, one feels a subtle impalpable metre pulsing. Some one possibly may be able to disentangle and define that metre; but I confess that I can't—simply because, each time I read, the *meaning* holds and fills my mind too full. Let a thing be said with such animation and directness that you try in vain to *think* of the form, then surely that form is perfect, whatever it is! The form vanishes in the meaning; and that is what our bodies will one day do —not disappear from sight, but so glow and be suffused in what they convey, as to cease to have any separate existence.[1]

There is no need, to-day, to justify Whitman's forms and rhythms, any more than there is need to justify those of Beethoven or Brahms or Wagner. There are good country folk who delight to sit and beat time with hand or foot to the village band; and there are folk who only recognise a ballad metre in poetry; but they need not detain us. Ballad metres have an excellent and charming use and

[1] "I had not dreamed," says Mrs. Gilchrist in *A Woman's Estimate of Walt Whitman*, "that words could cease to be words, and become electric streams like these. I do assure you that, strong as I am, I sometimes feel as if I had not bodily strength to read many of these poems. In the series headed 'Calamus,' for instance, in some of the 'Songs of Parting,' the 'Voice out of the Sea,' the poem beginning 'Tears, Tears,' &c., there is such a weight of emotion, such a tension of the heart, that mine refuses to beat under it—stands quite still—and I am obliged to lay the book down for a while."

quality, but they do not cover the whole ground.

There are two things in literature which demand expression—roughly, brain and heart. On the one hand, mere fact, description, argument; on the other, mood, emotion, mental colouring. As the extreme type of the one, we have books of law, science, mathematics; as the extreme type of the other, and lying beyond literature, music. In literature proper, there is always of course a blend or admixture of the two elements; but those works which express a predominance of the mental and scientific element come under the head of prose, and those which express predominant emotion come under the head of poetry and approach the musical in form. Just as in music every mood has its rhythm—light jingles of dances, lulling, swaying cradle-songs, ballad-refrains, swelling love-songs, strong marches, or great symphonic metres including these—so in poetry. "Wherever there is emotion concerned in the thought there will be emotional effects in the language—that is, there will be rhythm; and the wave-like rhythms and rhymes and recurrences will take on the simplest and briefest, or the most complex and far-reaching forms, according to the character of the emotion concerned."[1]

The underlying and dominant mood of Whitman's poems, corresponding to his theme, is extraordinarily vast and inclusive—and it requires for its expression a rhythm of similarly broad and flexible character. It is obvious that such emotions as he deals with could never be caged in a symmetrical verse or stanza.

> "I have not so much emulated the birds that musically sing,
> I have abandoned myself to flights, broad circles,

---

[1] "Angels' Wings," by E. Carpenter (1898), p. 73.

> The hawk, the sea-gull, have far more possess'd
> me than the canary or mocking-bird.
> I have not felt to warble and trill, however
> sweetly,
> I have felt to soar in freedom and in the fulness
> of power, joy, volition."

But in thus soaring in freedom and the fulness of power and joy he finds a rhythm and a music of his own. "I see," says Anne Gilchrist, "that no counting of syllables will reveal the mechanism of the music; and that this rushing spontaneity could not stay to bind itself with the fetters of [formal] metre. But I know that the music is there, and that I would not for something change ears with those who cannot hear it."[1]

Whitman needed for his expression a poetical form of the utmost flexibility—capable of adaptation to the widest ranges of his immense personality. It is, in fact,

[1] "A Woman's Estimate," now republished among the papers in "In *re* Walt Whitman" (McKay. Philadelphia, 1893).

his personality which forms the organic centre of "Leaves of Grass." He calls the latter (see "A Backward Glance o'er Travel'd Roads") "an attempt from first to last, to put *a Person*, a human being (myself, in the latter half of the Nineteenth Century, in America) freely, fully, and truly on record." As a work of art, therefore, "Leaves of Grass" ought to stand whole, unbroken, undivided, and grouped round the central presence of the author. "Who touches this, touches a man."—"In regard to the unity and construction of the poems," says John Burroughs in "The Flight of the Eagle,"[1] "the reader sooner or later discovers the true solution to be, that the dependence, cohesion, and final reconciliation of the whole are in the personality of the poet himself. . . . When Tennyson sends out a poem, it is perfect, like an apple or a

[1] "Birds and Poets" (New York, 1877), p. 234.

peach; slowly wrought out and dismissed, it drops from his boughs holding a conception or an idea that spheres it and makes it whole. It is completed, distinct, and separate—might be his, or might be any man's. It carries his quality, but it is a thing of itself, and centres and depends upon itself. Whether or not the world will hereafter consent, as in the past, to call only beautiful creations of this sort *Poems*, remains to be seen. But this is certainly not what Walt Whitman does, or aims to do, except in a few cases. He completes no poems, apart and separate from himself, and his pages abound in hints to that effect:—

> "'Let others finish specimens—I never finish specimens;
> I shower them by exhaustless laws, as Nature does, fresh and modern continually.'

His lines are pulsations, thrills, waves of force, indefinite dynamics, formless, constantly emanating from the living centre, and they carry the quality of the author's personal presence with them in a way that is unprecedented in literature."

And again Whitman says (I am quoting from the edition of 1860):—

> "I will not make poems with reference to parts,
> But I will make leaves, poems, poemets, songs, says, thoughts, with reference to ensemble;
> And I will not sing with reference to a day, but with reference to all days,
> And I will not make a poem, nor the least part of a poem, but has reference to the Soul,
> Because, having looked at the objects of the universe, I find there is no one, nor any particle of one, but has reference to the Soul."

The ultimate form therefore of Whitman's poems is the form of himself, of the Soul as individualised and uttered in him. As looking at the ocean, boundless and reaching far beyond our ken, we yet recognise in each wave the form of the sea which gives it birth; so in reading

"Leaves of Grass" we recognise in each poem or poemet the form and unifying law of the author. Indeed there is a singular resemblance in the great measured yet irregular roll of Whitman's lines to the onset of waves along a shore —now creeping white and low in long successive array, now madly surging and towering in spray, now lipping sunlit and blue upon the land. Every mood, at one time or another, is there and to be recognised—yet underneath, and greater than all, and illustrated by them all, the law and life of the ocean itself.

While all Whitman's poems are thus parts of a whole, and must gain their deepest meanings and interpretations through a study of the whole, there are some which are almost unintelligible *except* in this relation—mere ejaculations, single sentences, or not even so much as single sentences (see Kosmos, "Leaves of Grass," p. 303, also pp. 217, 218). Of these, Burroughs' remarks about their non-completion, except in relation to the poet's personality, are true in the most literal way. Of others, there is a decided sense of artistic completion in themselves, though still subsidiary to the total work. And it is interesting, with regard to this subject of form, to see how Whitman gains in these latter cases his artistic unity.

One of the most frequent and characteristic devices of his writing is the use of a very long sentence. By the phrasing of his lines the construction of a very lengthy sentence can be kept clear and effective, while the meaning and burden of it can be piled up and elaborated, till at last the total can be discharged upon the reader with overwhelming effect. Many of his poems (*e.g.* "When I heard the learn'd astronomer," p. 214; or, "I sit and look out," p. 215; or those two from *Children of Adam*, "Ages and ages returning," and "We too, how long we were fool'd," pp. 92 and 93), are constructed on this plan. They are just one single sentence, and convey one unitary effect. Others, though consisting of more than one sentence, are still the same in principle. Often by repeating the *form* of the sentence ("I see, I see;" "I hear, I hear"), he gains a like result. What a wonderful poem is that *Salut au Monde*, in which these sights and sounds, of the whole world, these lists and processions of earth-dwellers, these appeals to you, you, you, "whoever you are," pile up, in strange surging and swelling reiteration —till at last they break out and break down in the final four lines:—

> "Toward you all, in America's name,
> I raise high the perpendicular hand, I make the
> signal,
> To remain after me in sight for ever,
> For all the haunts and homes of men."

Here the picture of the immense earth, and the poet's relation to it, is the central motive. In another, the open road is the figure which holds all together. In another, the Brooklyn Ferry. In another, the broad axe. And in all, as I have said before, a deep pulsating music, easy to catch, though difficult to define.

Often the music is that of "recitative"—sonorous, bold, free, not returning into itself like a melody, but moving forward with suggestions of things to follow. This is perhaps the most general and characteristic of Whitman's musical effects. See, for instance, that strange poem :—

> "As Adam early in the morning,
> Walking forth from the bower refresh'd with sleep,
> Behold me where I pass, hear my voice, approach,
> Touch me, touch the palm of your hand to my
> body as I pass,
> Be not afraid of my body."

How finely that might be set to music—solemn, mystic, appealing, oracular! Or read "Old Ireland" (p. 284) in the same connection, and countless other poems or portions of poems. In the "Ox-tamer" (p. 307) there is much the same recitative effect, with more metrical return and melody. More rhythmical and melodic still is that beautiful "Vigil Strange," on p. 238, or the "Sight in Camp," p. 240; and more so still perhaps, the well-known "Come up from the fields, father," p. 236. In many of these we notice distinct refrains and recurrences, not only of lines, but of metres—often a return at the end to the refrain of the beginning, as in the "Ox-tamer" or the "March in the ranks hard prest," or "The bivouac's fitful flame"; often a recurrence throughout of a certain type of line—as of anapests (six-foot) in "Come up from the fields":—

> "But now from the fields come, father, come at the daughter's call,
> And come to the entry, mother, to the front door come right away,"

or some other sort of refrain, as in "Beat, Beat, Drums!" (p. 222), or in "Gods" (p. 213).

> "Lover divine and perfect comrade,
> Waiting content, invisible yet, but certain,
> Be thou my God."

Finally we have a few in distinct stanzas and set metre (or nearly so) like "O Captain" (p. 262), or "Pioneers" (p. 183), or the "Dirge for Two Veterans" (p. 246); but on the whole these are not the most characteristic or satisfactory of his pieces.

For short poems held together by a distinct mood and music of their own (even if the latter be hard to define), turn to "To Him that was Crucified," already quoted, or to "To a Common Prostitute," or to those wonderful lyric ejaculations "Tears" (p. 204), or "Darest thou now, O soul" (p. 338), or "The

Last Invocation" (p. 346), with their solemn organ-tones.

In two of his long poems, namely, "Out of the Cradle" (p. 196), and "When lilacs last in the door-yard bloomed," Whitman has by a combination of some of the devices above mentioned produced an artistic effect and unity which is very remarkable, and which has made these poems general favourites. The unitary scene and landscape in both cases, the recurrence of certain emblems, lilac and star and grey-brown bird or sagging moon and sea, the rhythmic songs introduced of love and death, and the sobbing melody of the surge throughout the first mentioned poem, and the repeated music of the Lincoln Hymn:—

> "O how shall I warble myself for the dead one there I loved?
> And how shall I deck my song for the large sweet soul that has gone?

> And what shall my perfume be for the grave of him I love?
>
> . . . . .
>
> Lilac and star and bird twined with the chant of my soul,"

—all these things give to these two great poems an artistic unity and distinction which single them somewhat out from the rest, and grant them (unlike some others of Whitman's) to stand alone as it were, and on their own merits.

Nevertheless it must be said, and somewhat in defence of John Burroughs' position, that these two poems, beautiful as they are, are not so characteristic, so deeply fascinating and impressive, so central in the whole scheme and cosmos of "Leaves of Grass," as those other great poems, which, though not so obviously metrical or artistically balanced and complete, are governed more directly by the presence and direct utterance of the personality behind them: I mean, of course, first and foremost, the "Song of Myself," and afterwards the two series, *Children of Adam* and *Calamus*, and such poems as "By Blue Ontario's Shore," "The Answerer" (p. 134), "The Sleepers" (p. 325), "To Think of Time" (p. 333), "Sunset" (p. 374), "Vocalism" (p. 297), "So Long" (p. 380), and many others. There is in these poems an extraordinary oracular prophetic utterance which lifts them right through the sphere of art, and out of it, into something above. "No one will get at my verses," he says,[1] "who insists upon viewing them as a literary performance, or attempt at such performance, or as aiming mainly towards art or aestheticism." It is in this quality in Whitman's work, transcending art, yet indeed only possible through the patient study, through the perfection and final surrender of art,

[1] See "A Backward Glance o'er Travel'd Roads," the prose Appendix to "Leaves of Grass" (Small, Maynard & Co., Boston, 1897).

that the secret of his power lies. In his poems of this order a technical unity is not demanded (though it may be found in some of them) because they speak in the name of that Self which is and remains the unity of all things—the wind which bloweth where it listeth over the world. They have no need to *seek* for unity and beauty, because in uttering the Self these things are already given and found. Here is a great mystery, difficult to express. No wonder that in that truly oracular poem, "Vocalism" (p. 297), Whitman announces so great, so almost terrifying and impossible an apprenticeship before "the divine power to speak words" can come and be loosened in man or woman—nothing less than the circling of all experience, and the final surrender:

> "For only at last after many years, after chastity, friendship, procreation, prudence and nakedness,

After treading ground and breasting river and lake,
After a loosen'd throat, after absorbing eras, temperaments, races, after knowledge, freedom, crimes,
After complete faith, after clarifyings, elevations, and removing obstructions,
After these and more, it is just possible there comes to a man, a woman, the divine power to speak words. . . .
Surely, whoever speaks to me in the right voice, him or her I shall follow,
As the water follows the moon, silently, with fluid steps, anywhere around the globe."

It is here no case of neglecting art; but technical art and all its devices are only a very very small part of the apprenticeship. Before the deep music and beauty of these greatest poems we can only stand silent, absorbing indeed, but in no mood to analyse. Something greater than mortal speaks to us in them, some voice blended of ages and ages and vistas of human experience. Something more even than human; for

Nature, the prairies and the lakes, the ocean and the forest by some hidden magic become vocal in them:

"I hear you whispering there, O stars of heaven,
O suns—O grass of graves—O perpetual transfers and promotions,
If you do not say anything how can I say anything?"

. . . . .

"The woodman that takes his axe and jug with him shall take me with him all day,
The farm-boy, ploughing in the field, feels good at the sound of my voice,
In vessels that sail my words sail, I go with fishermen and seamen and love them.

The soldier camp'd or upon the march is mine,
On the night ere the pending battle many seek me, and I do not fail them,
On that solemn night (it may be their last) those that know me seek me."

Whitman, by his vast command of and sympathy with the things of the actual world, by his strange interpenetration and identity with the elemental whole, has in these great poems revealed a presence which, as long as the waters glisten and the leaves rustle, can never pass or cease to speak to us; and as in ancient days, from some cavern on a mountain side, a voice in divine frenzy issuing was taken to be that of the Earth-god before whose eyes past and future are one, so from these writings the music arising seems to be the inspiration and part-utterance even of ageless Nature herself.

For the rest there are, of course, deficiences and weaknesses. As hinted earlier in this book, the voluminous power which marshals and holds in leash whole battalions of phrases, to hurl them finally on the reader with irresistible effect, sometimes fails; and then we get a lumbering, disjointed, efforted movement which is the reverse of admirable. Whitman's later poems, though interesting in many ways, do often show this deficiency of inspiration and some consequent lapse into mannerisms; and his prose perhaps shows the same more frequently.

To the reader coming to these works for the first time, the disregard of conventions in every direction is so great, that it sometimes attracts all his attention, rendering him insensible to the interior message, and annoying him with a suspicion of mere affectation. "If he only were not obscene," says such a reader, "or slangy, or prosaic, or contradictory; if he only would not put in lists of trades, or of seaport towns, or lines that ramble at large across all the proprieties of metre and grammar—we could endure him! But thus and thus he is intolerable." It is only after some familiarity and a gradual change of the point of view and perspective, that the reader begins to see that much which he thought affected is perfectly natural and in place. "To speak with the perfect rectitude and insouciance of the movements of animals, and the unimpeachableness of the sentiment of trees in the woods, and grass by the roadside," is Whitman's own standard, and the more one reads the more I think one is compelled to acknowledge his near approach to it. That he uses the parlance of common folk instead of the set phrases of the learned is not an affectation, but simply what Dante, and Chaucer, and Pushkin, and many another pioneer of a national literature has done; that he speaks freely of physiological things is not obscenity, but a deliverance from it; that his handling of facts appears prosaic or unemotional may easily arise from the reader's own want of association with the facts that are handled.

In all these cases of a new or unfamiliar style (as in painting or music) the interpretations do not yield themselves till the new point of view has been seized. Whitman has often been accused of want of humour — and it is notorious that nothing is more elusive and variable as between people and people — English, Scotch, French, German, American—than just this sense of humour. But no one who knows "Leaves of Grass" well can fail to detect the fund of quiet humour constantly flowing there beneath the surface. It has been said, No one with any sense of the comic could have written the lines :—

> "Now I absorb immortality and peace,
> I admire death, and *test propositions.*"

But does it follow that because a minor poet might fear to use such an expression, lest it should excite a smile, Whitman would also have been afraid, and have refused it, even though the expression exactly conveyed his meaning? And again, a phrase like "test propositions" may well appear comic at Oxford or Cambridge, and yet perfectly serene and sensible on an American prairie. These things are a little difficult to locate.

All the same it must be said that the poet does, in this way and at times, put a considerable strain upon his admirers! as when he writes:—

> "O setting sun! though the time has come,
> I still warble under you, if none else does, unmitigated adoration,"

or again—

> "I will report all heroism from an American point of view."

And there are affectations—or rather I think I should say, cases in which he has of set purpose adopted forms and attitudes not perfectly natural and spontaneous. For the most part his work is marvellously spontaneous, and, in its prophetic way, deriving at once from instinctive and subconscious regions; but there is no doubt (he says so himself) that in parts he "set himself" very deliberately to do certain things. And it is in these parts that I think he is least successful. Thus he set himself to vaunt and magnify "these States" in season and out of season (a good purpose in moderation, but rather overdone); to ignore all stock-poetic and classic forms and allusions whatever (a practice which cripples him at times), even to the extent of proscribing May and June in favour of Fifth-month and Sixth-month; and to coin and introduce if possible various hybrid and denationalised words, like Camerado, Santa Spirita, I exposé, and so forth (a matter in which he has often been anything but successful). These set efforts, which also appear sometimes in the *construction* of his poems, detract at such times from the winging singing quality of his work, and give a sense as of chains dragged along the ground.

Of these weaknesses and deficiencies, however, I must say that in the long-run they do not seem to me to bulk very largely. Though they may do so at first, and may seem serious, yet it is surprising how with continued reading they wane and lose their importance in the general splendour and adequacy of expression. And personally—with regard to the many quaint and outlandish things in Whitman—though they may cause a ripple in the mind, I find that they do not for me spoil the general effect, any more than for one sailing into New York harbour the splendid vista of shipping and shores is spoiled by the sight of a bottle or other such object borne on the blue and sunlit tide.

And when on the other hand one regards the extraordinary and admitted felicity and perfection of a vast number of his phrases, the absoluteness of the rendering and expression of some of the most difficult and subtle things, one sees that these quaintnesses, whatever may be their cause, certainly do not arise from lack of literary ability. The man who could write "the large unconscious scenery of my land with its lakes and forests," or " the gentle soft-born measureless light," or "dark mother always gliding near with soft feet," or "the yellow gold of the gorgeous, indolent, sinking sun, burning, expanding the air," was without doubt a master of expression. And I may conclude this paper with the words of Addington Symonds (" A Study of Walt Whitman," p. 150): " The countless clear and perfect phrases he invented, to match most delicate and evanescent moods of sensibility, to picture exquisite and broad effects of natural beauty, to call up poignant or elusive feelings, attest to his artistic faculty of using language as a vehicle for thought. They are hung, like golden medals of consummate workmanship and incised form, in rich clusters over every poem he produced. And, what he aimed at above all, these phrases are redolent of the very spirit of the emotions they suggest, communicate the breadth and largeness of the natural things they indicate, embody the essence of realities in living words which palpitate and burn for ever."

WALT WHITMAN'S CHILDREN

HENRY B. BINNS, in his "Life of Walt Whitman," lately published, discusses at some length the question of Whitman's paternity; and seems to arrive at the conclusion that the poet formed at least one relationship (this one probably at New Orleans in 1848) which led to the birth of a child or children.

Mr. Binns founds his discussion on an article of mine originally published in the *Reformer* (Feb. 1902); and, premising that in his book (pp. 51–3 and 349–50) he has added not a little to the evidence, I reprint the main portions of my article below, as follows:—

"In regard to Whitman's most personal and intimate relations there is curiously little known. Every one is aware that he was never married—that is, in any formal and acknowledged way. His life after the Civil War was clouded by intermittent paralysis, bringing with it invalidism and infirmity; and of his history before his arrival in Washington, *i.e.*, prior to the age of forty-four or so—the period when he would be most likely to knit up such relations—only the barest outline is known.

"'Leaves of Grass,' that extraordinary piece of self-revelation, gives us the mental attitude of the author. And perhaps (it may be said) we ought to be content with that; because if we know the mental and emotional attitude of a man we know the main thing. His external life and actions depend largely on accidental circumstances and conditions, his inner attitude is the expression of himself alone. 'Leaves of Grass' reveals to us a man, to whom the most intimate relations with his fellow men and women were familiar (at any rate in thought), and beautiful (at least in their proper time and place). The urge to closest contact appears everywhere through his poems: 'I sing the body electric'—'the body of my love, the body of the woman I love, the body of the man, the body of the earth.' He is not satisfied with communication through words and printed pages, or by the mere looking at photographic portraits:—

> "'Not words of routine this song of mine,
> But abruptly to question, to leap beyond yet nearer bring:
> This printed and bound book—but the printer and the printing-office boy?
> The well-taken photographs—but your wife or friend close and solid in your arms?'

"And in the poet's announcement and

summary of his own work, written by Whitman close after the issue of the first edition of 'Leaves of Grass,' he says of himself: 'Right and left he flings his arms, drawing men and women with undeniable love to his close embrace, loving the clasp of their hands, the touch of their necks and breasts, and the sound of their voices. All else seems to burn up under his fierce affection for persons.'

"It would not of course be reasonable to suppose that all the personal utterances, of acts done, of passions expressed, of experiences lived through, or of individuals loved—which are to be found in 'Leaves of Grass'—are to be taken as literal records of things which actually happened to the author himself. They could hardly be gathered into a single lifetime. Yet one can see that they are to be taken as experiences, *either* actual or potential, for which his inner spirit was prepared—

and as a record of things which he could freely accept, understand, and find place for. 'Through the period from 1837 to 1848,' says John Burroughs, 'without entering into particulars, it is enough to say that he sounded all experiences of life, with all their passions, pleasures, and abandonments. He was young, in perfect bodily condition, and had the city of New York and its ample opportunities around him. I trace this period in some of the poems in the *Children of Adam*, and occasionally in other parts of his book, including *Calamus*.[1] Certainly at times in these poems one can hardly avoid the conclusion that he is describing an actual bit of his own history—as in that poem :—

> '"Once I passed through a populous city imprinting my brain for future use with its shows, architecture, customs, traditions,

[1] John Burroughs, in "Walt Whitman : as Poet and Person." (New York, 1867.)

Yet now of all that city I remember only a
woman I casually met there, who detained
me for love of me,
Day by day and night by night we were together
—all else has long been forgotten by me.
I remember I say only that woman who passionately clung to me.
Again we wander, we love, we separate again;
Again she holds me by the hand, I must not go,
I see her close beside me with silent lips sad and
tremulous." '

"In a life so full and rich as Whitman's there must have been many such personal experiences, of which the world knows nothing, and will know nothing. He has himself told his friends that he had children—and in a letter to J. Addington Symonds (dated 19th August 1890), he mentioned that he had had six. Symonds writing to me in 1893 quoted the passage in question from this letter of Whitman's, and it runs as follows:—

"'My life, young manhood, mid-age, times South, &c., have been jolly bodily, and doubtless open to criticism. Though unmarried I have had six children—two are dead—one living Southern grandchild, fine boy, writes to me occasionally—circumstances (connected with their fortune and benefit) have separated me from intimate relations.'

"This is all, apparently, that the letter contained with reference to the fact of Whitman's paternity; but it is sufficient to establish the fact. Concerning the said children, and their mother, or mothers, there may be other evidence or information in existence; and if so, it would be interesting and important to elicit it.[1]

"I have heard people affirm their

[1] For some evidence that Whitman in his later years not unfrequently alluded to the fact of his fatherhood, see Binns' "Life of Whitman," p. 349. It is also supposed that, the lady at New Orleans being of aristocratic connection, her family would only recognise the children on condition of their fatherhood being concealed; and that these were the circumstances which separated Whitman "from intimate relations" with them.

'moral certainty' that Whitman never had any intimate relations with women, and that all the expressions in 'Leaves of Grass' which seem to point that way, are merely Platonic, or fanciful, or allegorical —but it is not very easy to see on what such 'moral certainty' could in any case be founded; and in the face of the above extract from Whitman's own letter, it would certainly have to be abandoned.

"On the other hand it would be a rash, and I think a wrong conclusion to suppose that because Whitman had several children (out of the bounds of formal marriage) he was therefore a dissolute and uncontrolled person, much given to casual *liaisons* with the opposite sex. We know nothing, as I have said, of the circumstances which led to these connections, nor have we the material for passing any judgment of the kind referred to—even if we were so disposed. We know at any rate that in his later life Walt was singularly discreet, almost reserved, in his relations with women; and in that very interesting interview with Pete Doyle, which is given by Dr. Bucke in his edition of Whitman's letters to Pete[1]— one of the best running accounts of Walt which we have, though of course quite *extempore*—Pete says in one passage:—'I never knew a case of Walt's being bothered up by a woman. In fact, he had nothing special to do with any woman, except Mrs. O'Connor and Mrs. Burroughs. His dispositon was different. Woman in that sense never came into his head.'

"Though there are points in the interpretation of this passage which are not quite clear, it at any rate conveys the impression of Whitman's reserve

[1] "Calamus: A Series of Letters," &c. (Small, Maynard & Co. Boston, 1897.)

towards the other sex; and seems in one part to suggest that his 'disposition' was unfavorable to close relations with women.[1]

"Pete's view in either case may appear a little difficult to reconcile with the six children; but then we must remember that the inception of the latter and the 'times South' of Whitman's letter would belong to an early date—including probably his visit to New Orleans in 1848–49—before he was thirty years of age. And the Whitman of that time might well differ somewhat in disposition from the Whitman of twenty years later when Pete knew him.

[1] In a conversation reported by Horace Traubel ("In *re* Walt Whitman," p. 34), George Whitman, the poet's brother, seems to take much the same general view as Pete. He says: "Although I am asked that question, I am confident I never knew Walt to fall in love with young girls, or even to show them marked attention. He did not seem to affect the girls."

"That Whitman was not by any means insensible to the charms of the fair sex, even in this later period, is indicated by the following extract (dated October 1868), from one of his own letters to Pete—though it will be seen that there is a certain histrionic air about the passage which suggests that it should not be taken *too* seriously:—'I also made love to the women, and flatter myself that I created at least one impression—wretch and gay deceiver that I am. The truth is, Peter, that I am here at the present time mainly in the midst of female women, some of them young and jolly, and meet them most every evening in company; and the way in which this aged party comes up to the scratch and cuts out the youthful parties and fills their hearts with envy is absolutely a caution.'

"Pete Doyle was one of Walt's dearest friends—perhaps his dearest; and Walt's letters to Pete are veritable love-letters. The story of their meeting, as given by Pete in his 'interview' is quite romantic: 'It is a curious story. We felt to each other at once. I was a conductor (on a tram). The night was very stormy—he had been over to see Burroughs before he came down to take the car—the storm was awful. Walt had his blanket—it was thrown round his shoulders—he seemed like an old sea-captain. He was the only passenger, it was a lonely night, so I thought I would go in and talk with him. Something in me made me do it, and something in him drew me that way. He used to say there was something in me had the same effect on him. Anyway I went into the car. We were familiar at once—I put my hand on his knee—we understood. He did not get out at the end of the trip—in fact went all the way back with me. I think the year of this was 1866. From that time on we were the biggest sort of friends.'

"Their intimacy, as shown by the correspondence, lasted on undiminished for over ten years. Through the letters peep in and out the forms and names of other friends, mostly young fellows, tram-conductors, fire-engine men, &c., to whom Walt sends his love and messages. His devotion to his friends of this kind, the 'bus-drivers in early days in New York, the ferry-men, the soldiers in the war, and others, is of course well known; and it appears to have been in many cases ardently returned. 'Many a soldier's kiss dwells on these bearded lips.' In fact, in his poems we find his expressions of love towards men and towards women put practically on an equality—if anything indeed the references to the former are the more frequent and the more passionate. In actual life, too, during that later period after the war, there can be no doubt that his intimacies with men were much more numerous and close than with women. We have no record, I think, during that time, of any very close intimacy with a woman, though of warm friendships with women we have several instances.

"Summing up then all that has been said, I gather that in his early years Walt had some *liaisons* with the fair sex; certainly one such relation, which may have lasted several years, and which may (see the already quoted poem) have been chiefly initiated and pressed from the lady's side; but that in his later period (after the age of forty-five or so)—whether from a change of temperament or any other cause—these ceased to play a part in his life; at any rate there is no indication of them. It is clear also that throughout his life his intimacies with men were very close and ardent;

and it seems possible that these, in the later period, to some extent supplied the deficiency on the other side.

"Walt's attitude in 'Leaves of Grass' towards men or women is, as I have already remarked, singularly uniform. Both sexes seem to come equally within the scope of his love. And there is a passage in Pete Doyle's already quoted interview which curiously corroborates this. Pete probably never read 'Leaves of Grass,' or took much account of it; but he gives the following from his own observation: 'Towards women generally Walt had a good way—he very easily attracted them. But he did that with men, too. And it was an irresistible attraction. I've had many tell me—men and women. He had an easy gentle way—the same for all, no matter who they were, or what their sex.'

"Whether this large attitude towards

sex, this embrace which seems to reach equally to the male and the female, indicates a higher development of humanity than we are accustomed to—a type supervirile, and so far above the ordinary man and woman that it looks upon both with equal eyes; or whether it merely indicates a personal peculiarity; this and many other questions collateral to the subject I have not touched upon. It has not been my object in making these remarks to enter into any vague speculations, but rather to limit myself to a few conclusions which seemed clear and obvious and fairly demonstrable."

Allen & Co. Sc.

R. W. Emerson
about the year 1855 (Age 52)

WHITMAN AND EMERSON

THE relations between Whitman and Emerson form an interesting subject. There is little doubt that the two men had a deep mutual respect and admiration for each other; and however any chance expression dropped at any time, on either side, might seem to belie this, I believe it lasted to the end. It is quite likely that Whitman owed something in the inception of "Leaves of Grass" to Emerson's writings. This does not mean of course that, without Emerson, Whitman would have failed of his work; but, as so often happens in such cases, when a mass of material is forming somewhat undefinedly, and seeking outlet, the work of the predecessor comes to give it a decisive touch, and bring it to birth.

In his very interesting "Reminiscences of Walt Whitman" (originally printed in the *Atlantic Monthly*, February 1902[1]), John Townsend Trowbridge touches on this subject; and without endorsing his remarks in every particular, it may be interesting to quote them. Relating a conversation he had with Whitman one Sunday at Boston, in the spring of 1860, when Whitman had come over to Boston to see his third edition through the press, Trowbridge says:—

"I was extremely interested to know how far the influence of our greatest writer (Emerson) had been felt in the making of a book which, without being

[1] Now substantially reproduced in his book, "My Own Story."

at all imitative, was pitched in the very highest key of self-reliance. In his letter to Emerson, printed in the second edition of 'Leaves of Grass,' speaking of 'Individuality, that new moral American continent,' Whitman had averred: 'Those shores you found; I say, you led the States there—have led me there.' And it seemed hardly possible that the first determined attempt to cast into literature a complete man, with all his pride and passions, should have been made by one whose feet were not already firmly planted on 'those shores.' Then there was the significant fact of his having mailed a copy of his first edition to Emerson.

"Whitman talked frankly on the subject, that day on Prospect Hill, and told how he became acquainted with Emerson's writings. He was at work as a carpenter (his father's trade before him) in Brooklyn, building with his own hands

Walt

and on his own account small and very plain houses for laboring men; as soon as one was finished and sold, beginning another,—houses of two or three rooms. This was in 1854; he was then thirty-five years old. He lived at home with his mother; going off to his work in the morning and returning at night, carrying his dinner-pail like any common laborer. Along with his pail he usually carried a book, between which and his solitary meal he would divide his nooning. Once the book chanced to be a volume of Emerson; and from that time he took with him no other writer. His half-formed purpose, his vague aspirations, all that had lain smouldering so long within him, waiting to be fired, rushed into flame at the touch of those electric words,—the words that burn in the prose-poem 'Nature,' and in the essays on 'Spiritual Laws,' the 'Oversoul,' 'Self-reliance.' The sturdy carpenter in his working-day garb, seated on his pile of boards; a poet in that rude disguise, as yet but dimly conscious of his powers; in one hand the sandwich put up for him by his good mother, his other hand holding open the volume that revealed to him his greatness and his destiny—this is the picture which his simple narrative called up, that Sunday so long ago, and which has never faded from my memory.

"He freely admitted that he could never have written his poems if he had not first 'come to himself,' and that Emerson helped him to 'find himself.' I asked if he thought that he would have come to himself without that help. He said, 'Yes, but it would have taken longer.' And he used this characteristic expression: 'I was simmering, simmering, simmering; Emerson brought me to a boil.'

"It was in that summer of 1854, while he was still at work upon his houses, that he began the 'Leaves of Grass,' which he wrote, and rewrote, and re-rewrote (to quote again his own words), and afterwards set in type with his own hand.

"I make this statement thus explicit because a question of profound personal and literary interest is involved, and because it is claimed by some of the later friends of Whitman that he wrote his first 'Leaves of Grass' before he had read Emerson. When they urge his own authority for their contention, I can only reply that he told me distinctly the contrary, when his memory was fresher.

"The Emersonian influence is often clearly traceable in Whitman's early poems; seldom in the later. It is in the first line of the very first poem in which he struck the keynote of his defiant chant: 'I celebrate myself.' Yet the form Whitman chose for his message was as independent of Emerson's as of all other literary forms whatsoever."

One of the "later friends" to whom Trowbridge refers is no doubt John Burroughs, who on page 16 of his "Walt Whitman as Poet and Person" (New York, 1867) says, speaking of the first edition of "Leaves of Grass":—

"I take occasion to say that Whitman, up to the time he published the quarto edition, here mentioned, had never read the 'Essays' or 'Poems' of Mr. Emerson at all. This is positively true. In the summer following that publication, he first became acquainted with the 'Essays' in this wise: He was frequently in the habit of going down to the sea-shore at Coney Island, and spending the day bathing in the surf and rambling along the shore, or lounging on the sand; and on one of these excursions he put a volume of Emerson into the little basket containing his dinner and his towel. There, for the first, he read 'Nature,' &c. Soon, on similar excursions, the two other volumes followed. Two years still elapsed, however, and after his second edition was issued, before he read Mr. Emerson's poems."

It is interesting, in these two quotations, to find the incident of the Emerson volume in the dinner-basket repeated, yet placed by one writer in the year 1854, and by the other, equally decisively in 1856! The matter is not extremely important; but it illustrates the extreme and eternal difficulty of getting reliable historical evidence. In this case there are three memories, either of which may be at fault, and one of which *must* be—Whitman's, Trowbridge's, and Burroughs'. Did Whitman, in forgetfulness, give to Burroughs, sometime between '63 and

'67, a different account from what he gave to Trowbridge in '60? or did either Burroughs or Trowbridge only imperfectly remember the account he heard? It is difficult to say. Whitman in his quite late years seems to have adopted the Burroughs views; but Whitman's memory in his later years became very unreliable. In his "Backward Glance o'er Travel'd Roads" (published in 1888) he says, speaking of the importance of the Secession War in his own life and thought, that "Without those three or four years and the experiences they gave, 'Leaves of Grass' would not now be existing"; and that although he had "made a start before," the beginnings of "Leaves of Grass" might — except for this — have come to naught, "almost positively would have come to naught." This, considering that far the larger and more important part of "Leaves of Grass" was already printed and *published* in the 1860 edition, a year or more before the war broke out, is rather disconcerting; and suggests that his memory may have been equally at fault with regard to Emerson's part in "Leaves of Grass," as it was with regard to the part played by the war.

I say the matter is not very important; because it is obvious that whatever part Emerson's teaching played it was only a small part and of brief duration. It may very possibly only have come in after a start of some kind had already been made on "Leaves of Grass" (see letter quoted, *infra*, p. 186); it certainly had nothing to do with the long "foreground" of Whitman's early life on farms, in cities, and by the sea-shore, where the book was really prepared; nor anything to do with the special developments of the poems, as in *Children of Adam*, or their literary style — things which Emerson distinctly disapproved of. At the same time it seems to me quite likely that at some moment the magnificent intellectual intuitive outlook of Emerson, as of an eagle in high-soaring vision of seas and continents, sweeping the whole world into the compass of his thought, did give to Whitman just what he might have been waiting for (though probably in any case it would have come to him some time), the magic touch and inspiration which set his kosmos in order. No doubt an outside push of some kind is often required for the launching of a big ship. On the whole the evidence brought forward by Trowbridge seems to me to favour his case—the fact of Whitman's sending a copy of his *first* edition to Emerson (showing that he already thought something of Emerson's opinion), his printed letter to Emerson in the second edition, "those shores you found . . . have led me there," his addressing Emerson as "Master" in the same letter, and so on. In the "Notes left over" of "Specimen Days" (p. 321) Whitman himself says: "The reminiscence that years ago I began like most youngsters to have a touch (though it came late, and was only on the surface) of Emerson on the brain—that I read his writings, and addressed him in print as 'Master,' and for a month or so thought of him as such—I retain not only with composure, but positive satisfaction. I have noticed that most young people of eager minds pass through this stage of exercise."

With regard to Emerson's opinion about the new poems at this period, it is clear from his letter of July 21, 1855, to Whitman: "Dear Sir,—I am not blind to the worth of the wonderful gift of 'Leaves of Grass.' I find it the most extraordinary piece of wit and wisdom that America has yet contributed," &c.,—it is very clear, I say, that Emerson was greatly impressed, and indeed delighted, with the volume. With his clear and piercing vision he seems to have at once (or in a wonderfully brief time) reached through the odd rough husk to the sweet and precious kernel of the book; and for this as well as for his hearty expressions of appreciation the world must ever be grateful to him. Nevertheless the book, as was inevitable, roused in him queer doubts and heart-searchings. Either in 1855 or in the early part of 1856 Emerson called twice upon Whitman; and though in these visits the foundation of a personal friendship was laid, it is clear that they revealed also great gulfs of difference. Emerson could not quite stomach Walt Whitman, the rough, with his invasively democratic ways, nor see anything particularly interesting in his working-folk chums and pals; while Whitman, on the other hand, found his visitor too literary and intellectual. On the occasion of my own visit to the States in 1877, I stayed a night at Emerson's house at Concord—most pleasantly and hospitably received—and enjoyed greatly his talk as we walked up and down the old-fashioned garden, or sat in his book-lined study. When I spoke of Whitman, and asked what he thought of him, he laughed (a little nervously, I thought) and said, "Well, I thought he had some merit at one time: there was a good deal of promise in his first edition—but he is a wayward, fanciful man.[1] I saw him in New York, and asked him to dine at my

[1] I am here simply transcribing notes made a few days after the interview. He used a third epithet beside wayward and fanciful, something like "violent," but I hardly think it was so strong as that. (See *supra*, p. 48.)

hotel. He shouted for a 'tin mug' for his beer. Then he had a noisy fire-engine society. And he took me there, and was like a boy over it, as if there had never been such a thing before!" He went on, in words which I do not recall, to object to the absence of metre in "Leaves of Grass"; and ended, I remember, by taking down a volume of Tennyson from the shelf—handling it affectionately and showing me the author's autograph on the fly-leaf—and dwelling on the beauty of the Tennysonian diction and metre.[1]

[1] I may as well here transcribe my further notes of Emerson's personal appearance at the time, as follows: "Emerson's failure of memory for names is quite painful [his age was then 74], and there is the fixed look of age in his eye, yet he is active in body and full of fun and enjoyment of intellectual life. His eyes are greyish blue, the corners of his lips are often drawn upward, and there is a wonderful bird-like look about the face, enhanced by his way of jerking his head forward as he speaks. His eyes sometimes look very straight and intense: and then comes a moonlight smile over the face, very charming. His domestic life seems admirable."

These few words about Whitman, spoken by Emerson to a casual visitor, must of course not be given too much weight, or supposed to represent his total and final estimate. But I insert them here, as they probably represent pretty fairly certain points of difference and even disagreement which he discovered on personal acquaintance. On further reading, too, doubtless Emerson felt that he could not corroborate or justify a great deal of the matter, as well as the metre, of "Leaves of Grass." He was probably swayed to and fro by various currents of feeling with regard to it, and could not settle clearly in his mind what he did think. This is illustrated by a letter he wrote to Thomas Carlyle in 1856, to accompany a copy of the book, which he was sending:—

"One book, last summer, came out in New York, a nondescript monster, which yet had terrible eyes and buffalo strength, and was indisputably American—which I thought to send you; but the book throve so badly with the few to whom I showed it, and wanted good morals so much, that I never did. Yet I believe now again, I shall. It is called 'Leaves of Grass,'—was written and printed by a journeyman printer in Brooklyn, New York, named Walter Whitman; and after you have looked into it, if you think, as you may, that it is only an auctioneer's inventory of a warehouse, you can light your pipe with it."

It could only have been a few weeks after the above letter had been written to Carlyle about the first "Leaves of Grass," that—quite unexpectedly to Emerson—a second edition of the book appeared, with Emerson's complete letter of 21st July 1855, printed in an Appendix, and an extract from the same letter, "I greet you at the beginning of a great career," in gold upon the cover! Besides this, there was a long reply-letter from Whitman to Emerson, addressing the latter as "Master," and containing the above-quoted passages about "those shores you found," &c.

Whitman has been often blamed for this quite unauthorised use of Emerson's letter—and certainly according to our Cis-Atlantic literary codes it was a cool thing to do: very cool—considering of course that in this second edition were many pieces that Emerson had never even seen! But though the act may be difficult to defend, it must be remembered that public opinion and practice on the other side of the water was and is decidedly more lax and easy-going in such matters than on this side. Whitman probably failed to realise (it was hardly his nature to do so), the reaction this advertisement might have upon Emerson and *his* interests. He was thinking of his own bantling first edition, flouted, scorned, neglected, and like to perish, and of the splendid testimony from one of the greatest of living names in letters, which would suddenly lift it into fields of life and light. "I supposed the letter was meant to be blazoned,"—he said one day to Trowbridge—"I regarded it as the chart of an emperor." It did not occur to him that its blazoning might possibly cost the emperor his throne!

But indeed the matter was serious, comically serious. Here was Emerson, the imperial one, whose finger laid on a book was like a lighthouse beam to all the coteries of Boston, actually recommending some new poems to the whole world in terms of unstinted praise. The whole world, of course, went to buy them. A hundred parlors of mildly literary folk or primly polite Unitarian and Congregational circles beheld scenes over which kind history has drawn a veil! —the good husband or head of the house, after tea or supper, settling down in his chair, "Now for the new book, so warmly spoken of!" The ladies taking their knitting and sewing, their dresses rustling slightly as they arrange themselves to listen, the general atmosphere of propriety and selectness; and then the reading! Oh, the reading! The odd words, the unusual phrases, the jumbled sequences, the stumbling uncertainty of the reader, the wonderment on the faces of the listeners, and finally—confusion and the pit! the book closed, and hasty flight and dispersion of the meeting. Then, later, timid glances again at the dreadful volume, only to find, amid quagmires and swamps, the reptilian author addressing the belovèd Emerson as "Master," and saying, "these shores *you* found!" Was it a nightmare? Had the emperor gone mad? or was his printed letter merely a fraud and a forgery?

One can imagine the annoyance all this caused to Emerson himself—the deluge of letters and inquiries, the whirlpools of controversy among his myriad followers, the would-be champions who gaged their word and everlasting destiny on his entire innocence, &c. Truly the throne rocked for a season. But it was too well based to be upset. Indeed I cannot but think that Emerson, with his sterling good sense and mental solidity, rather enjoyed it all at bottom—the uproar, the searchings of heart, and the confusion of his congregations and coteries (whose narrowness and provincialism were often a trial to him). In his heart of hearts—though doubtless he thought Whitman had played him unfair, and though certainly he did not think Whitman's manner of speech on sexual questions either wise or gracious—still I believe he must have recognised and did at that time recognise that the book, "Leaves of Grass," was a tremendous gain to the world, and that it was even going to do pioneer work for him, Emerson, along his own line.

I think I am right in saying that there was no public retaliation by Emerson against the author of the offending book. I have, at any rate, not heard of any. There was, however, considerable public stir against it. It was savagely criticised, and "so extreme was the feeling excited by it, that some good people in New York seriously contemplated having the author indicted and tried for publishing on obscene book."[1] The publishers, Fowler & Wells, fearing injury to their

[1] See Bucke's "Walt Whitman," p. 141.

business, threw the book up; and so after a brief career its publication ceased, and for the next four years it remained as a thing dead.

It was in 1860 that Emerson and Whitman met again. Whitman had come to Boston to superintend the printing of a third edition, to be issued by Thayer and Eldridge. Heroic, calm, and undaunted, unresentful even of neglect, he simply went on his way. If the first and second editions of "Leaves of Grass" had aroused opposition, the third was still more likely to do so. It gathered together many of the most offending poems, with new ones of the same character, in two groups, *Children of Adam*, and *Calamus*, which were certain to attract attention. It was bold indeed of Thayer and Eldridge to undertake the publication. Whether by any chance one of the firm may have persuaded Emerson to intervene with the author, in favour of a general toning down of the book, I know not. But it is certain that Emerson came to see him, and taking him out onto Boston Common, walked with him for two hours discussing this very subject. Of that memorable conversation Whitman must speak for himself. In "Specimen Days," p. 191, under date 10–13 Oct. 1881, he says: "Up and down this breadth by Beacon Street, between these same old elms, I walked for two hours, of a bright sharp February midday twenty-one years ago, with Emerson, then in his prime, keen, physically and morally magnetic, arm'd at every point, and when he chose wielding the emotional just as well as the intellectual. During those two hours he was the talker and I the listener. It was an argument, statement, reconnoitring, review, attack, and pressing home (like an army corps in order, artillery, cavalry, infantry), of all that could be said against that part (and a main part) in the construction of my poems, *Children of Adam*. More precious than gold to me that dissertation. It afforded me, ever after, this strange and paradoxical lesson; each point of Emerson's statement was unanswerable, no judge's charge ever more complete or convincing, I could never hear the points better put—and then I felt down in my soul the clear and unmistakable conviction to disobey all, and pursue my own way. 'What have you to say then to such things?' said Emerson, pausing in conclusion. 'Only that while I can't answer them at all, I feel more settled than ever to adhere to my own theory, and exemplify it,' was my candid response. Whereupon we went and had a good dinner at the American House. And thenceforward I never wavered or was touched with qualms (as I confess I had been two or three times before)."

Very fine is this scene between the two men. Emerson bearing no grudge against the buffalo poet, candidly doing his best to give "Leaves of Grass" its proper scope, and save it (as he thought) from its own indiscretions—Whitman, loyal to himself and to Emerson, equally candidly refusing to budge. A hearty dinner afterwards, and separation with mutual respect.[1]

It is probable that for the next twenty years the two friends did not see each other. I find no evidence of their meeting. The war broke out; Whitman went

[1] In a letter to W. D. O'Connor (see New York *Tribune*, 18th June 1882) Whitman wrote, "What made and ever makes the argument of Emerson in that walk on the Common dear and holy to me was its personal affectionateness, as of an elder brother to a younger. It was a vehement and even passionate well-wishing, which I felt then, and feel to this hour, the gratitude and reverence of my life could never repay." (W. S. Kennedy's "Reminiscences of Walt Whitman," p. 77.)

south and remained at Washington, and afterwards at Camden, New Jersey, with only occasional and brief visits to New York. There was not much chance or likelihood of their meeting. Nevertheless their communications were not broken, and the elder man had not ceased to be interested in the younger; for we find, according to Trowbridge, that in November 1863, Whitman (who was then looking about for some official work or post at Washington) had by him two letters of recommendation written by Emerson—the one to Senator Sumner, and the other to Secretary Chase. Of what other correspondence or meetings there may have been between them for the next twenty years, we do not hear much.[1] Emerson's

[1] Emerson seems to have helped Whitman in the matter of hospital funds; and the two appear to have just seen each other at the re-burial of Poe at Baltimore in 1875. (See Binns' "Life of Whitman," pp. 198 and 258.)

respect for "Leaves of Grass" as a feasible contribution to literature seems to have waned. He respected of course much of the matter of it, but could not stomach the manner. He told his friend Sanborn once that the book read like "a mixture of the *Bhagvat-Gita* and the *New York Herald*."[1] He included no specimen of it in his collection "Parnassus" (1874); and detested its metre or want of metre.[2] [Whitman says somewhere—"Specimen Days," p. 321—"I see he covertly or plainly likes best superb verbal polish, or something old or odd—Waller's 'Go, lovely rose,' or Lovelace's lines 'To Lucasta'—and the like."] Yet for the Man, as well as I think for his Message in its real essence, Emerson had a great and enduring respect.

[1] "Reminiscences of Walt Whitman," by W. S. Kennedy (1896), p. 78.

[2] Nevertheless Emerson himself at an earlier age had made experiments in the same direction.

In 1881 Walt came once more to Boston to superintend a new edition of his poems. Since 1860 much had happened. The first two editions (1855 and 1856) had been scouted by the public and hastily dropped by the publishers; the 1860 edition fell almost dead through the War. Walt Whitman went to Washington. It was not till 1867 that he printed a fourth edition (New York), including "Drum Taps." The fifth came in 1871 (Washington). The sixth in 1876 (centennial and author's edition, Camden) in two volumes, including prose. And the seventh is the one of which we are speaking (Osgood & Co. Boston, 1881–2). Hardly was the book out, and selling well, when the Society for the Suppression of Vice in Boston pounced. The Attorney-general for Massachusetts, through the District Attorney, served a notice on Osgoods (early in '82). Osgoods appealed to Whitman to withdraw some of the poems. Whitman absolutely refused; and once more the publishers threw the book up and left the edition on his hands!

But to return to our subject. Emerson of course was not ignorant of the stir that was being made. Indeed there can be little doubt that both by his own family and from outside he was urged to dissociate himself from the book and its author. But he was not going to do anything of the kind.[1] In September 1881, Whitman came over from Boston (from his proof-reading) to stay a night with Sanborn at Concord. Emerson (now quite an old man, seventy-eight) and

[1] "The true fact is, R. W. Emerson had a firm and deep attachment to Whitman from first to last, as person and poet, which Emerson's family and several of his conventional literary friends tried their best in vain to dislodge." (See W. S. Kennedy's "Reminiscences of Walt Whitman," p. 77.)

other friends came in for the evening—"a long and blessed evening" Walt calls it ("Specimen Days," p. 189). He describes in fact how, without being rude, he was able to take a good look at Emerson most of the time, and speaks of "the well-known expression of sweetness in his face, and the old clear-peering aspect quite the same." Then the next day, Sunday, the Emersons asked *him* to dinner. "Several hours at Emerson's house, and dinner there. An old familiar house (he has been in it thirty-five years), with surroundings, furnishments, roominess, and plain elegance and fulness, signifying democratic ease, sufficient opulence, and an admirable old-fashioned simplicity: modern luxury, with its mere sumptuousness and affectation, either touched lightly upon or ignored altogether. Dinner the same. Of course the best of the occasion

(Sunday, Sept. 18, '81) was the sight of Emerson himself."

This dinner and hearty reception by Emerson Whitman looked back upon with something like pride, as a "victor-event" in his life. (See letter of 1887 to W. S. Kennedy, p. 76 of his book.) The next year, May 6, 1882, he stood by Emerson's grave. "How shall I henceforth dwell on the blessed hours when, not long since, I saw that benignant face, the clear eyes, the silently smiling mouth, the form yet upright in its great age—to the very last, with so much spring and cheeriness, and such an absence of decrepitude that even the term *venerable* hardly seemed fitting. . . . We can say, as Abraham Lincoln at Gettysburg, It is not we who come to consecrate the dead—we reverently come to receive, if so it may be, some consecration to ourselves and daily work from him." ("Specimen Days," p. 197.)

With these words we may leave the personal relation between the two men. The nobility of them both, the grandeur, sincerity, and simplicity of their relation, the hearty accord, affection, and admiration, beneath grave and acknowledged differences of habit and opinion—all make up a picture of deep and lasting significance, and one which future ages can hardly fail to cherish. On the purely literary side, however, it was perhaps only natural that, as time went on, they should distinctly drift apart. Emerson was less and less able to adapt himself to Whitman's strange new departures. Whitman more and more avowedly separated his respect for the man from his respect for the writer. In latest years he seemed almost anxious that he should *not* be thought to have learnt anything from Emerson's books. In the letter already alluded to, of 1887, to W. S. Kennedy, he says: "It is of no importance whether I had read Emerson before starting 'Leaves of Grass' or not. The fact happens to be positively that I had *not;*"[1] and later in the same letter: "If I were to unbosom to you in the matter I should say that I never cared so very much for Emerson's writings, prose or poems, but from his first personal visit and two hours with me . . . I had a strange attachment and love for *him* and his contact, talk, company, magnetism." In Whitman's "Specimen Days," also (pp. 321–2) he has some keen criticisms of the

[1] This letter is odd and jumbley and a little confusing in style, and I must say (considering also its date) does not carry entire conviction to me.

"bloodless intellectuality" and other defects of Emerson's style — criticisms which, though decidedly good on the whole, seem to me needlessly stringent, and even a bit captious in parts.

THE END

Printed by BALLANTYNE, HANSON & Co.
Edinburgh & London

Also by EDWARD CARPENTER

The Art of Creation

Essays on the Self and its Powers

Crown 8vo, Cloth, gilt top, 266 pp. 5s. net.

The Book is an attempt to explain the Creative process in the light of modern (and ancient) thought. It suggests—as the title would indicate—that the Creation of the World, like a work of Art, proceeds by perfectly definite laws from inner states of being and feeling to outer manifestation; and that Man himself, as soon as he understands, can take part in this art of creation. The book is both theoretical and practical. In its pages there is a reconcilement of Spirit and Matter, of Plato and Darwin, of Religion and Physiology, of the Gods and Evolution; and the chapters on Creation and Transformation lead on to the development of the highest orders of knowledge and power in mankind.

Manchester Guardian.—"Written with great simplicity and charm, and no thoughtful reader who takes it up will fail to find interest and profit in it.

LONDON: GEORGE ALLEN

Other Works by the same Author

TOWARDS DEMOCRACY: Complete Poems. Library Edition, 1905, cloth, gilt edge, 506 pages, 3s. 6d. net.

THE SAME, Pocket Edition, India paper, with limp binding and gilt edge, 3s. 6d. net.

ENGLAND'S IDEAL and other Papers on Social Subjects. Fourth Edition, 1902, 176 pages, cloth, 2s. 6d.; paper, 1s.

CIVILISATION: ITS CAUSE AND CURE, essays on Modern Science, &c. Eighth Edition, 1906, 176 pages, cloth, 2s. 6d.; paper, 1s.

LOVE'S COMING OF AGE: a series of papers on the Relations of the Sexes. Fourth Edition, 1903, 168 pages, cloth, 3s. 6d. net.

ANGELS' WINGS: Essays on Art and Life, with nine full-page plates, cloth gilt, 248 pages, 6s.

ADAM'S PEAK TO ELEPHANTA: sketches in Ceylon and India. New Edition, 1903, cloth gilt, 4s. 6d.

THE STORY OF EROS AND PSYCHE, with first book of Homer's Iliad done into English, and frontispiece, cloth gilt, 2s. 6d.

IOLÄUS: An Anthology of Friendship. Printed in red and black inks, with ornamental initials and side notes; cloth, gilt edge, 2s. 6d. net.

CHANTS OF LABOUR: a Songbook for the People, edited by EDWARD CARPENTER. With frontispiece and cover by WALTER CRANE. Paper, 1s.

AN UNKNOWN PEOPLE: pamphlet on intermediate types of men and women, price 6d. net.

PRISONS, POLICE, AND PUNISHMENT: an Inquiry into the Causes and Treatment of Crime and Criminals. Crown 8vo, cloth, 2s. net.

EDWARD CARPENTER: THE MAN AND HIS MESSAGE. Pamphlet by TOM SWAN, with two portraits and copious extracts from the above works, price 6d. net.